LOOKING UP

Images to Uplift and Inspire

Photographs
by

Herman Chan

First Edition

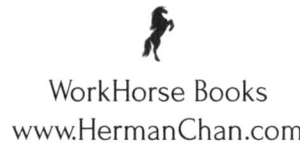

WorkHorse Books
www.HermanChan.com

First Edition, 2014, manufactured in USA
1 2 3 4 5 6 7 8 9 10 LSI 20 19 18 17 16 15 14

Photograph of Herman Chan on the "About the Author" page was taken by Bill Winters
[www.billwinters.com]

All other photographs appearing in this book taken by Herman Chan.

Cover and book layout by Michael Linnard

Print: ISBN: 978-0-9913381-3-9

First Edition

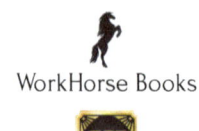

WorkHorse Books

www.HermanChan.com

FOREWORD

As a real estate expert and media personality, I am fortunate to get booked to speak at industry events and conferences across the nation. I am so grateful I get to share my helpful, hilarious nature to anyone who will listen! My topics of choice are technology, branding, messaging, and social media. Connecting to a live audience, making them laugh and learn, that's my real passion. All along, I always thought I was teaching them. But I was wrong. Sometimes they teach me.

You see, since high school I was an amateur shutterbug, snapping photos where ever I went, usually of architecture, properties and decor. I didn't think much of it and just did it for myself really. But one day at a speaking engagement, a real estate agent came up to me before I hit the stage and she said "Herman, I love, love, love your photos. Keep doing what you are doing." I quickly thanked her but she pressed on. She was hospitalized for a long time and lost her clientele. Even as her weight went up and her health went down, she took solace in my photos. I asked her why on earth she would do that? After all, they are just Instagram pics from my iPhone. She replied, "Everyone shoots down and close up. Their kids, their food, their pets. Herman, your photos always look up. They're uplifting. I see the big picture." I was rushed onto stage before I could really process her comment. I never got her name but I was touched. Images really do affect people. They can be visual words of encouragement. Ergo, that's why I entitled this book "Looking Up."

Things are never as bad as they seem. Always look up!

—Herman Chan

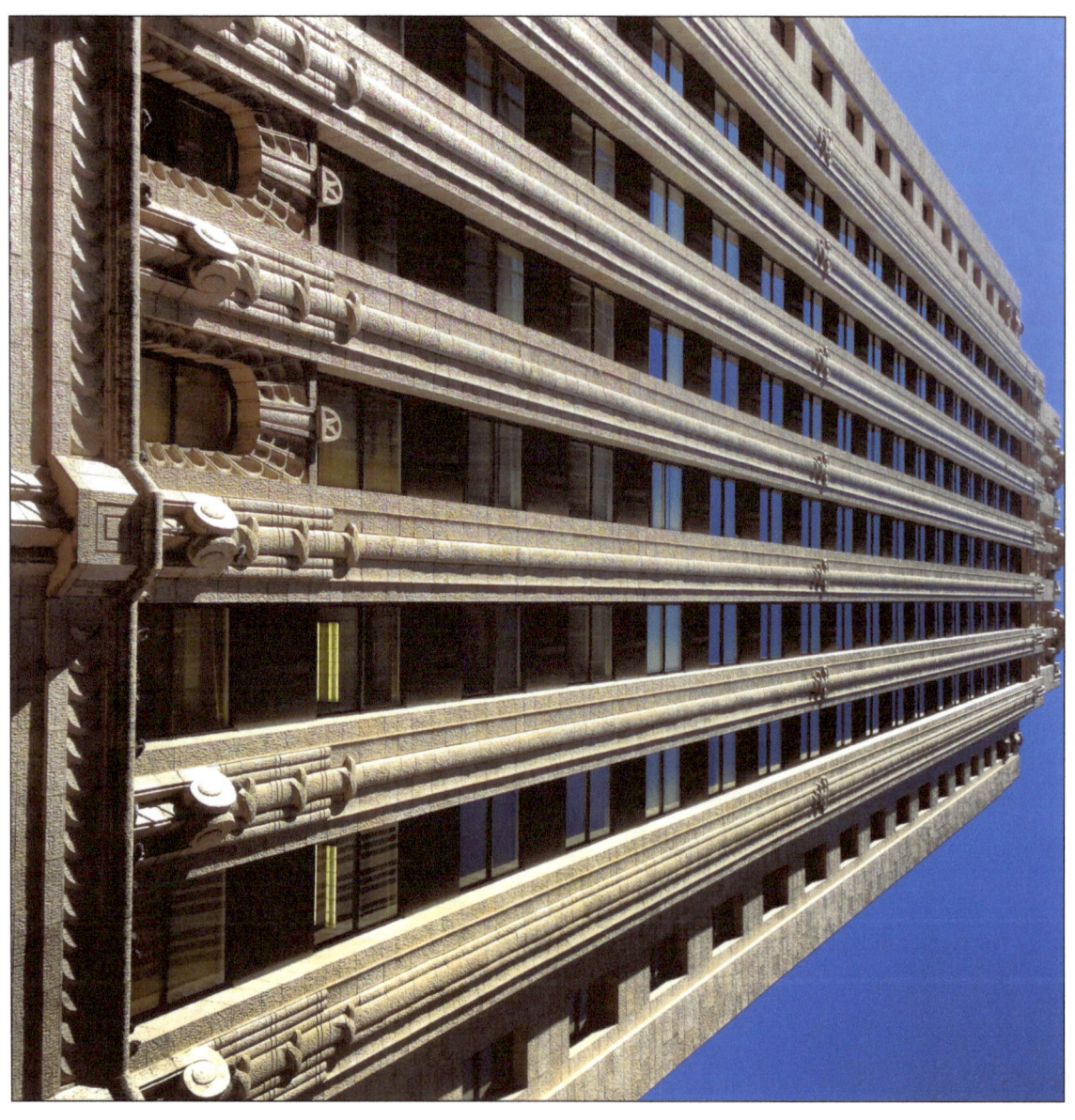

L: Financial District, San Francisco.
R: Noe & Market Street, San Francisco.

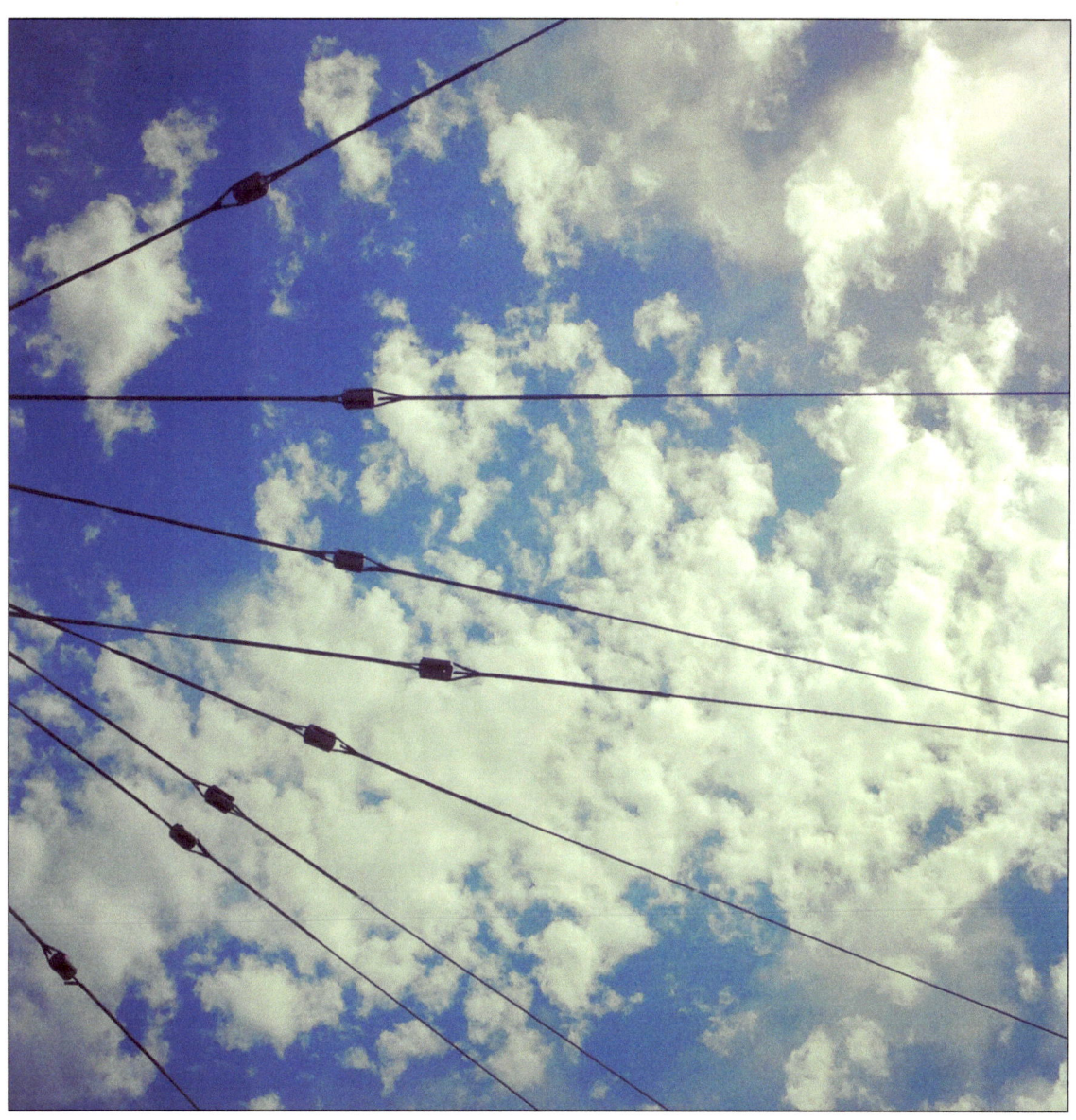

Always be a first-rate version of yourself, instead of a
second-rate version of somebody else.

—Judy Garland

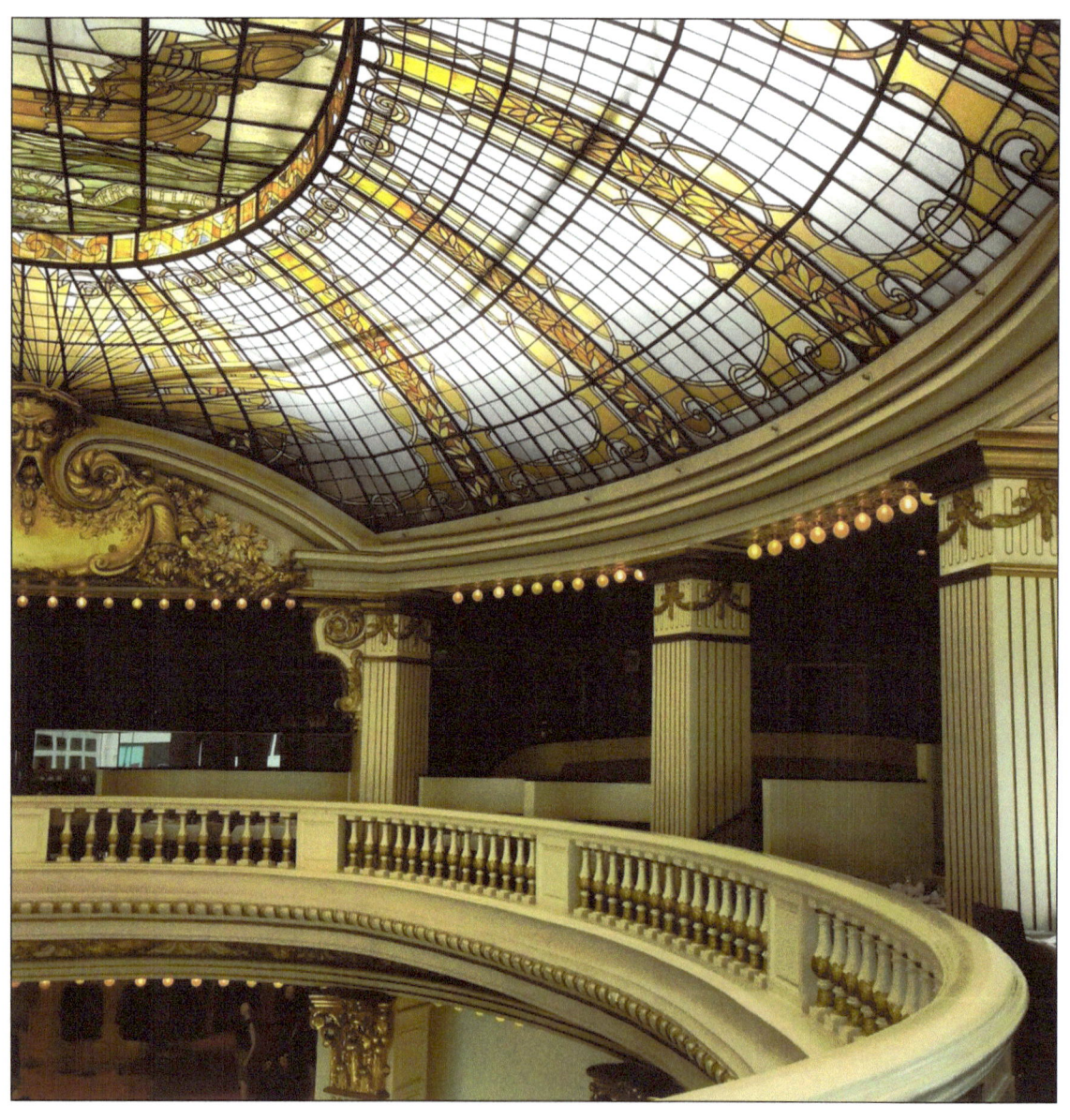

L: Rotunda Restaurant, Nieman Marcus.
R: Los Angeles Theatre Center.

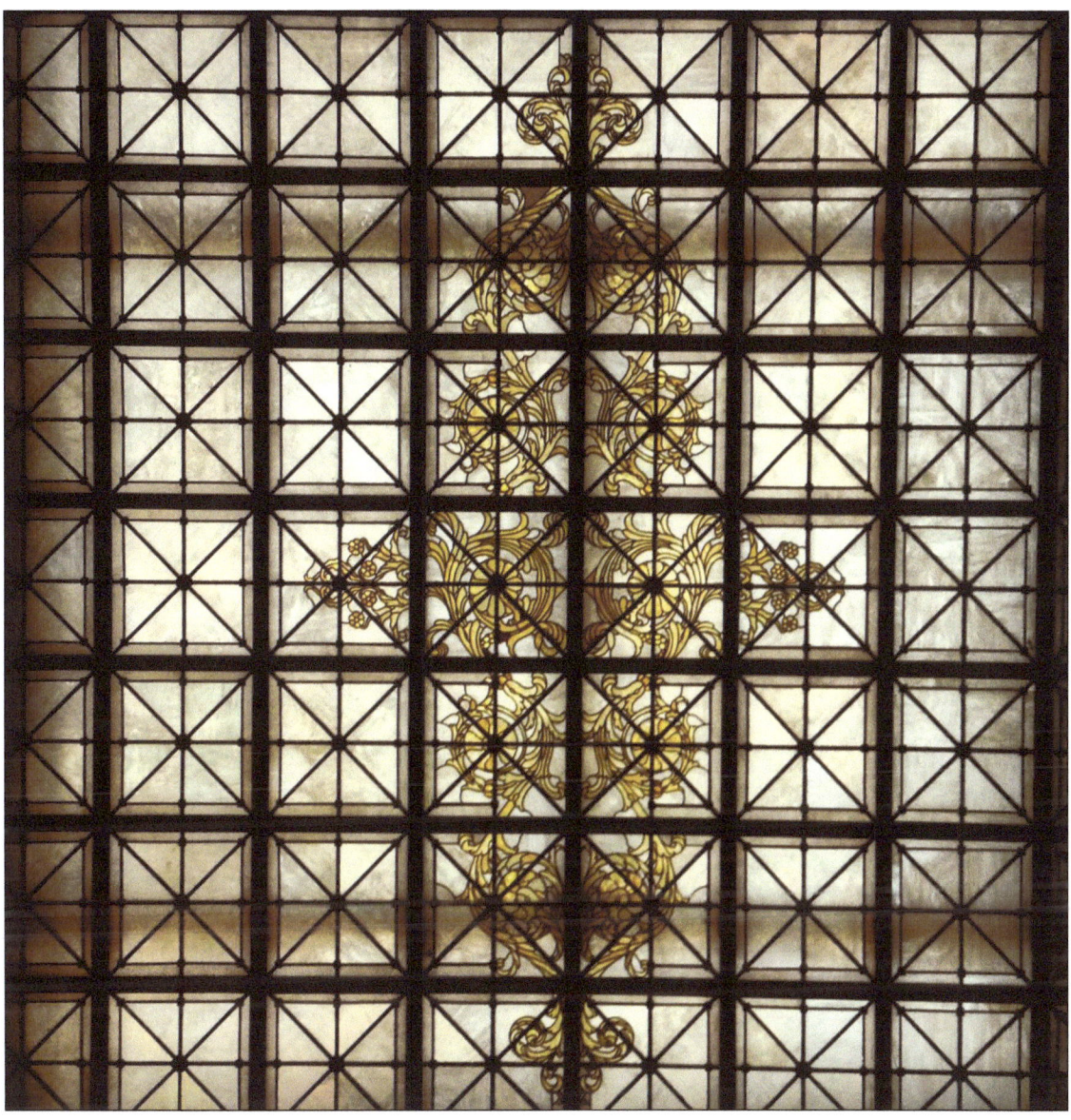

People are like stained-glass windows. They sparkle and shine
when the sun is out, but when the darkness sets in, their true
beauty is revealed only if there is a light from within.

—Elizabeth Kübler-Ross

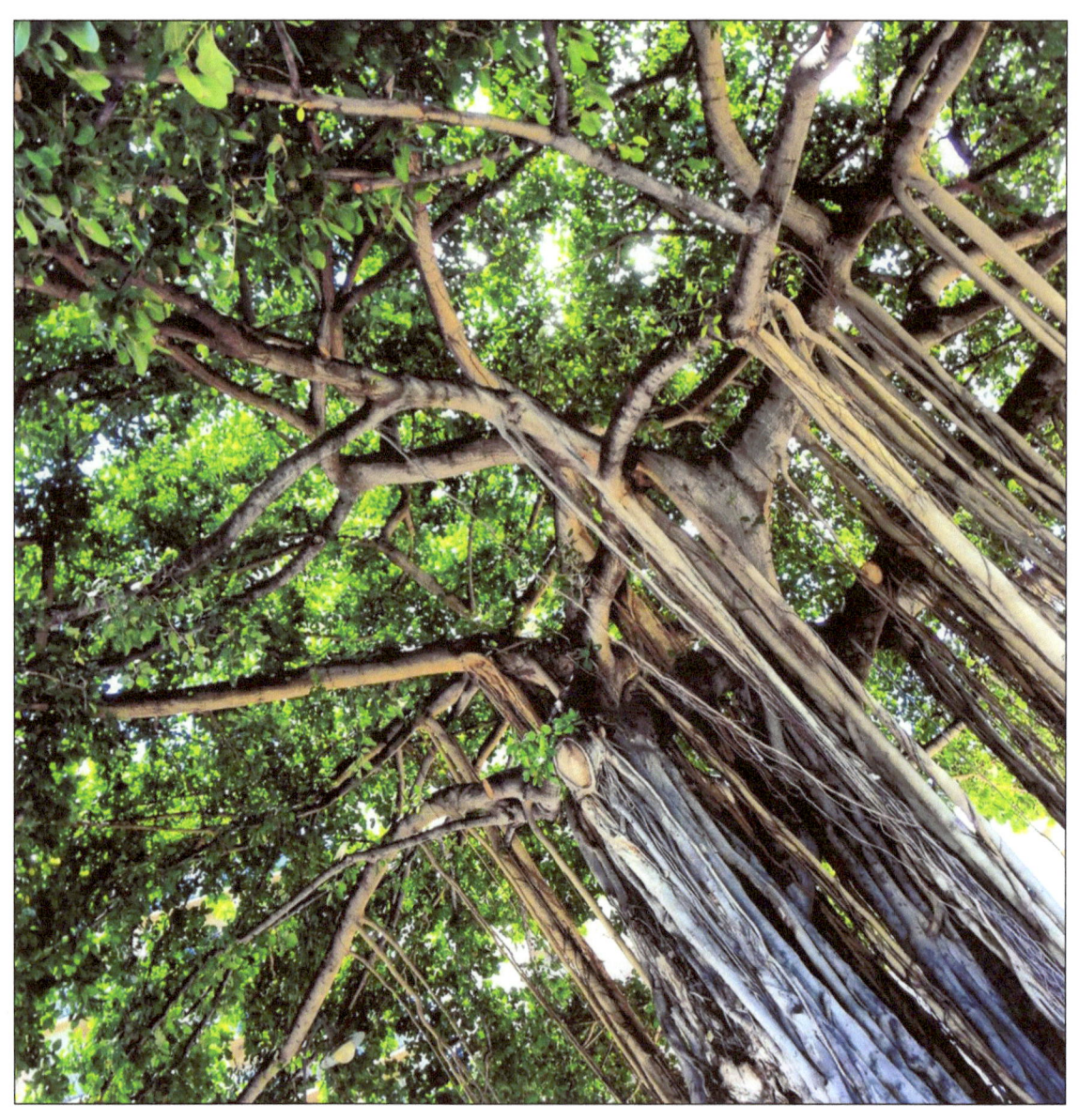

L: Waikiki, Hawaii.
R: Philz Coffee, Berkeley, California.

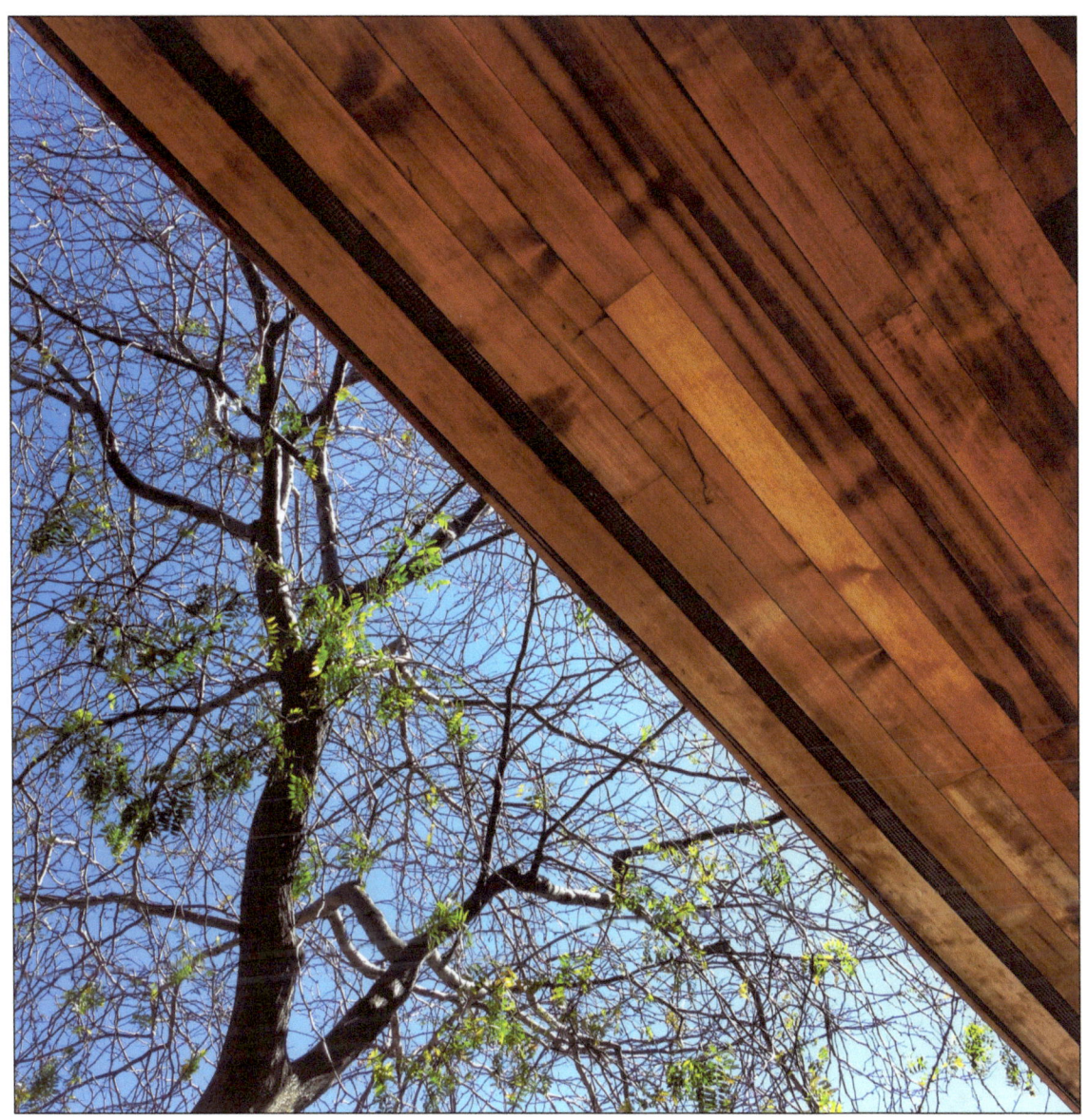

The road to success is always under construction.

—Lily Tomlin

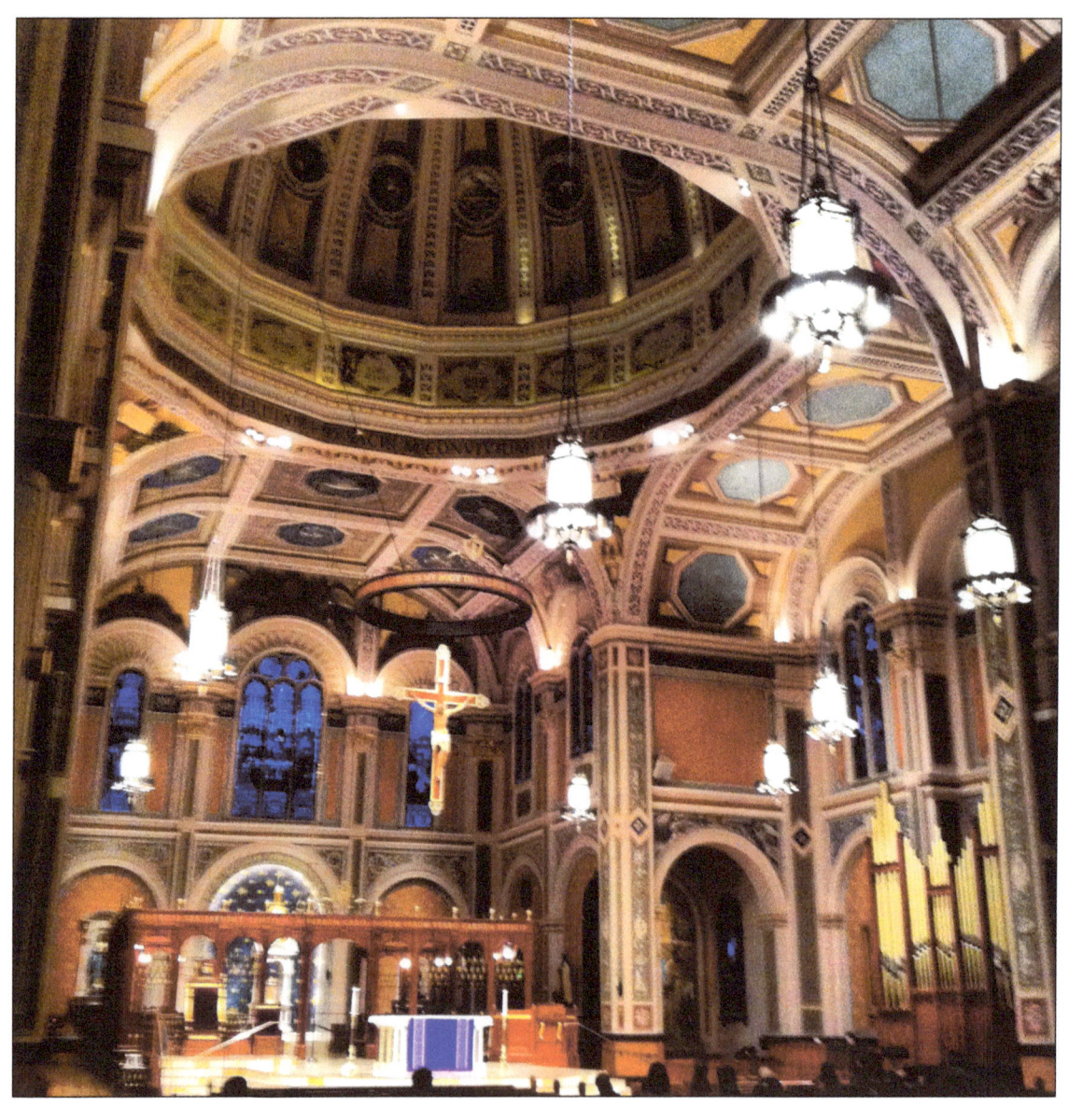

L: 1870s Cathedral of the Blessed, Sacramento.
R: New Transbay Terminal, San Francisco.

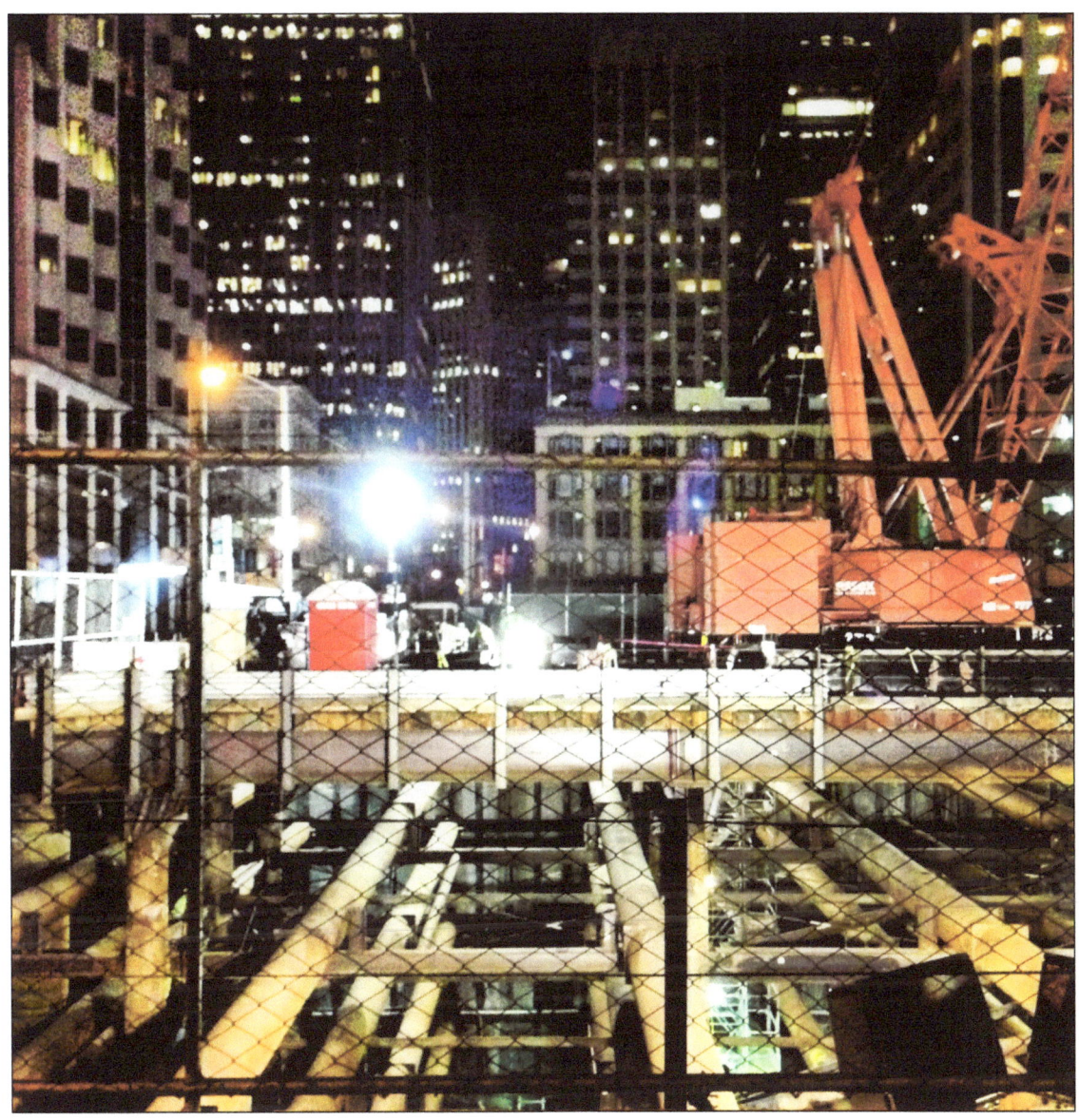

Architecture is the reaching out for the truth.

—Louis Kahn

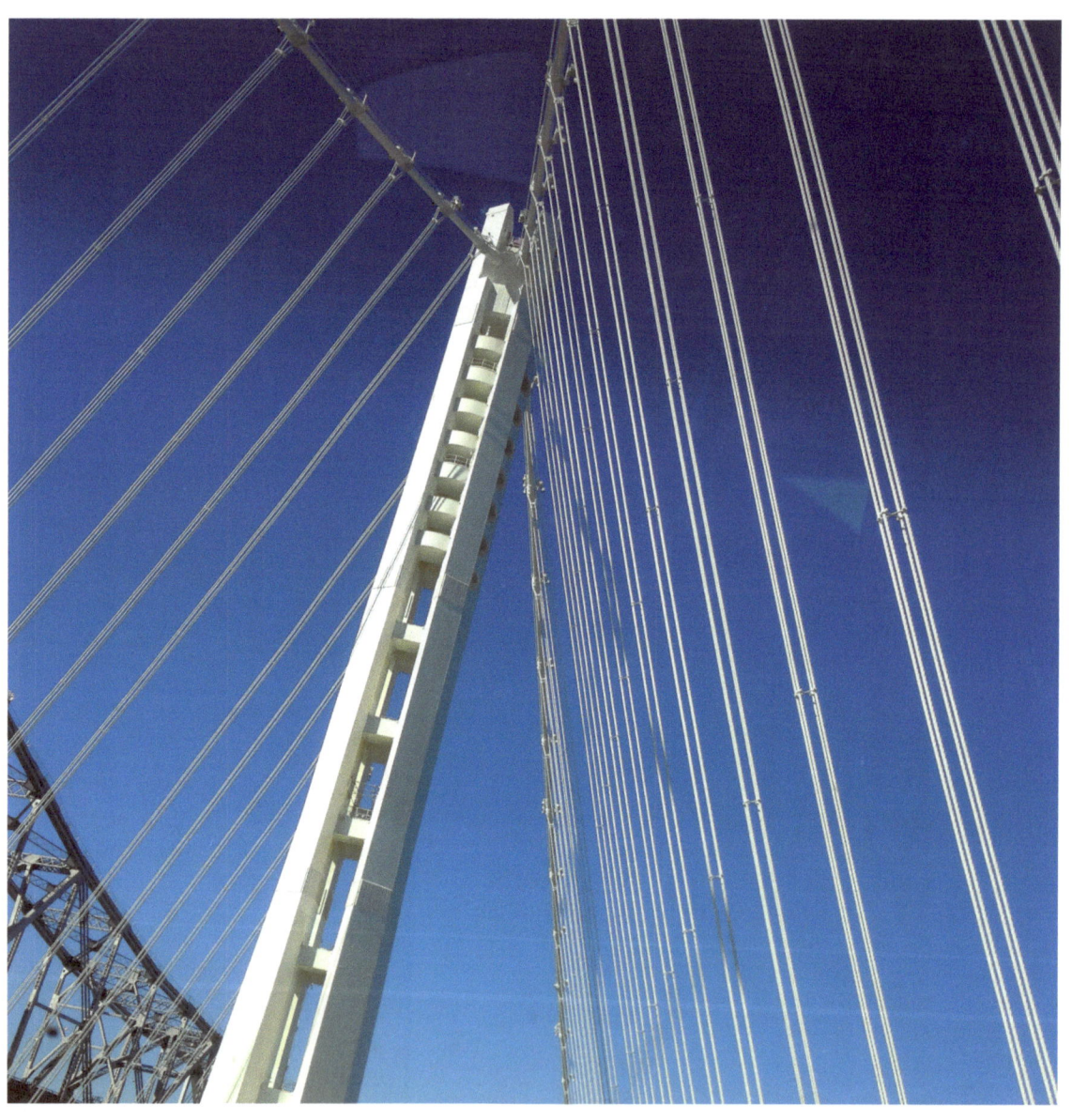

L: Willie Brown Bridge
R: ...AKA the Bay Bridge.

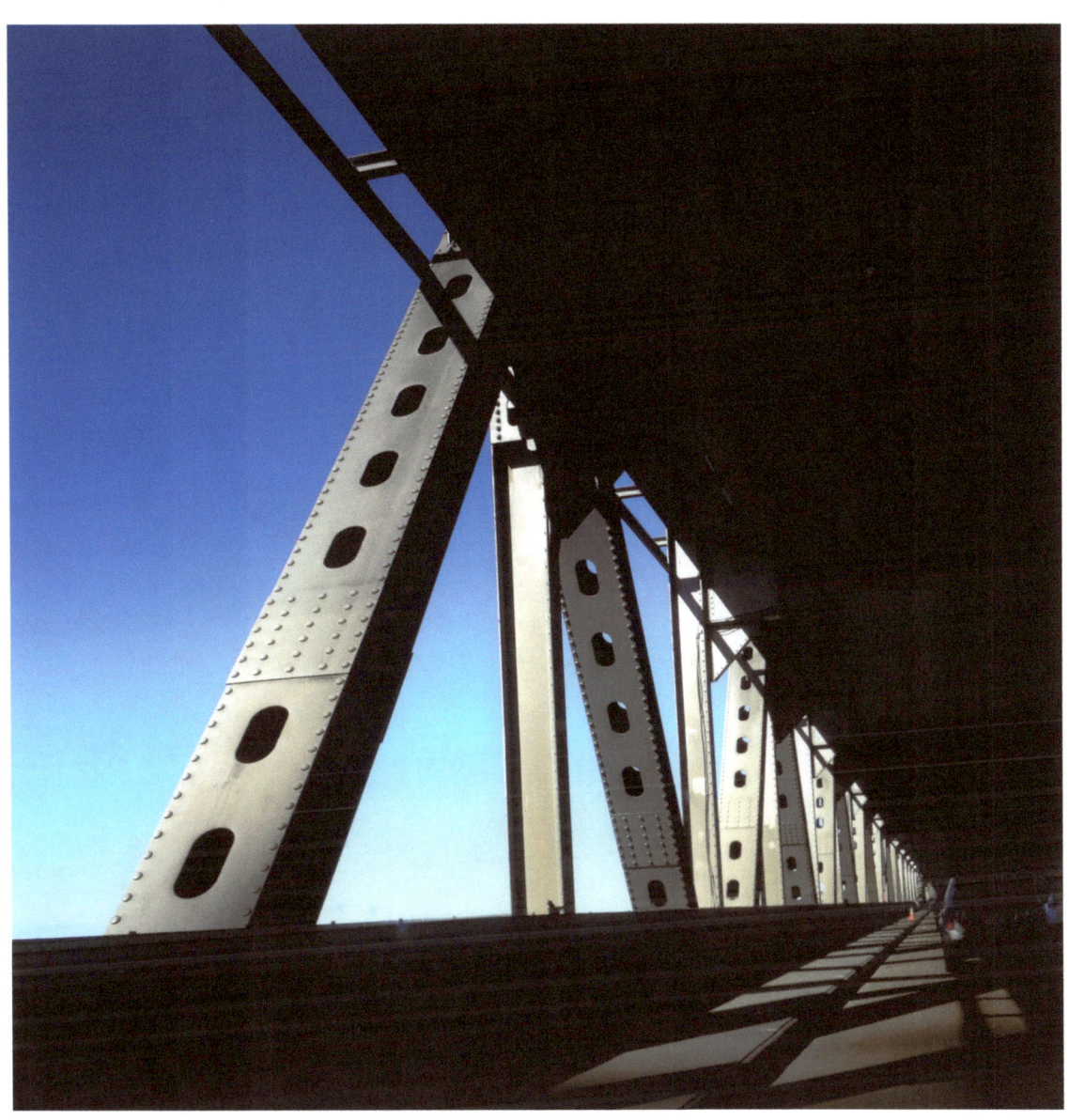

Do not allow people to dim your shine because they are blinded. Tell them to put on some sunglasses, cuz we were born this way, bitch!

—Lady Gaga

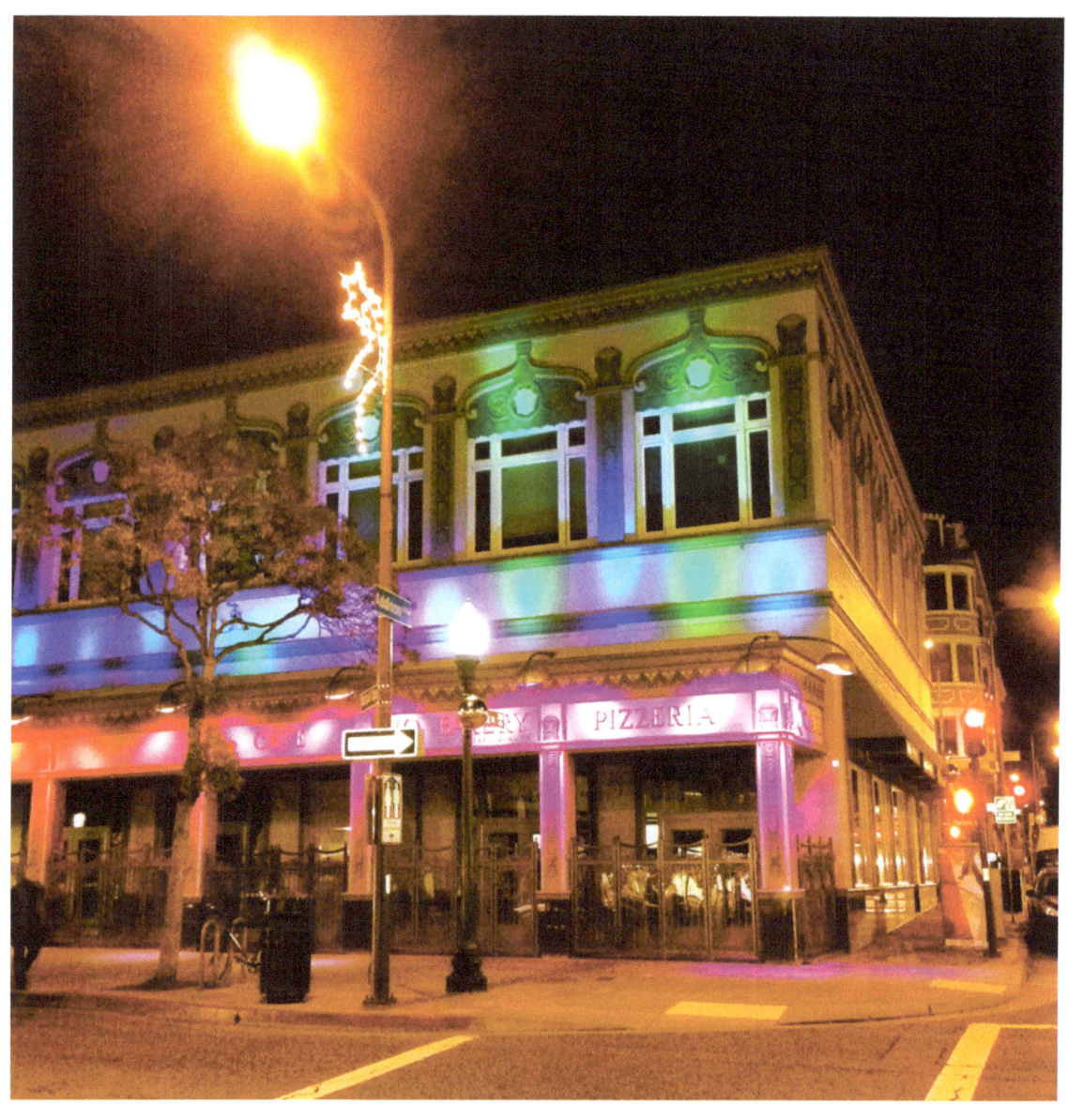

L: Downtown Berkeley.
R: Downtown Sacramento.

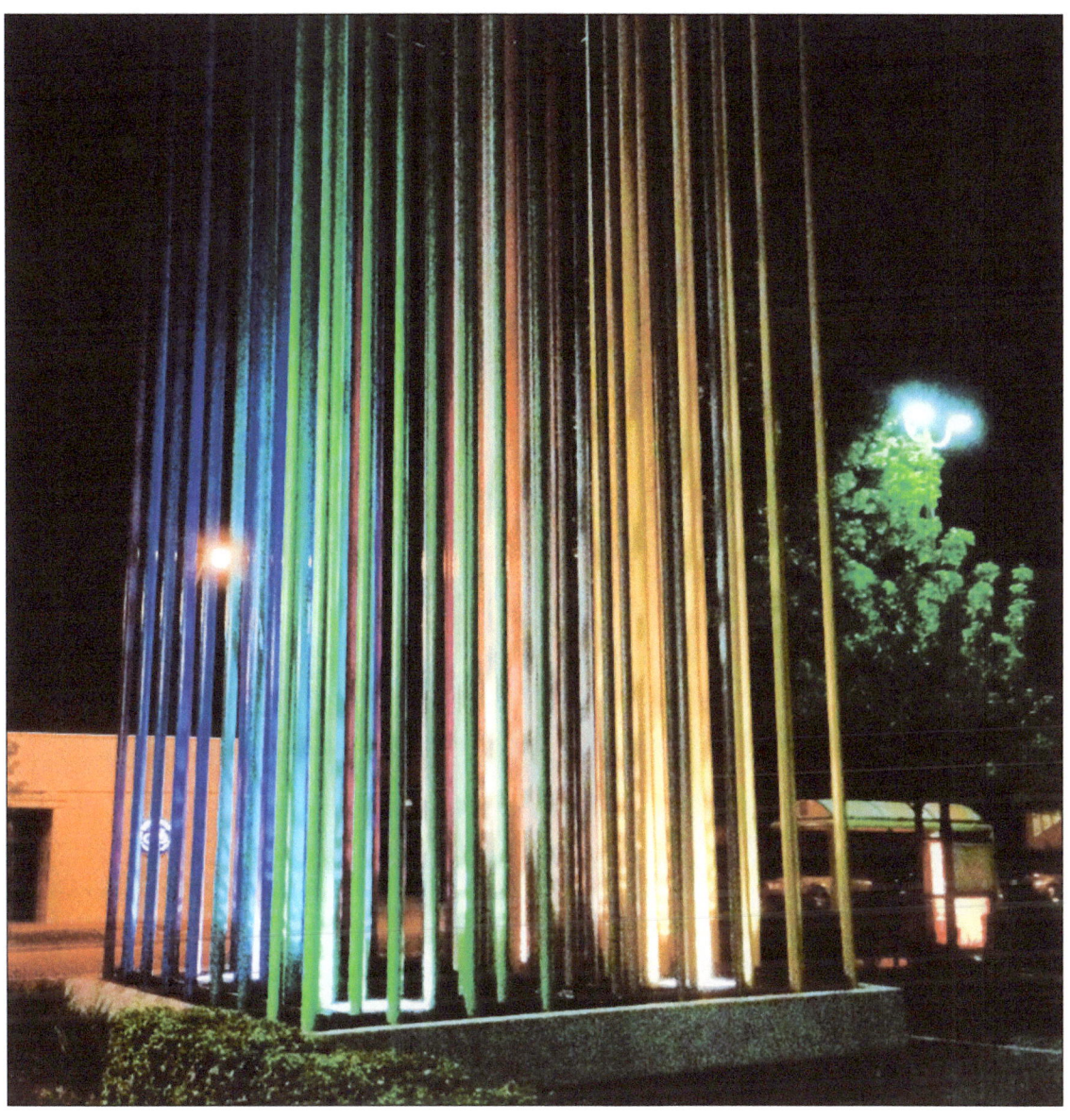

The way I see it, if you want the rainbow,
you gotta put up with the rain.

—Dolly Parton

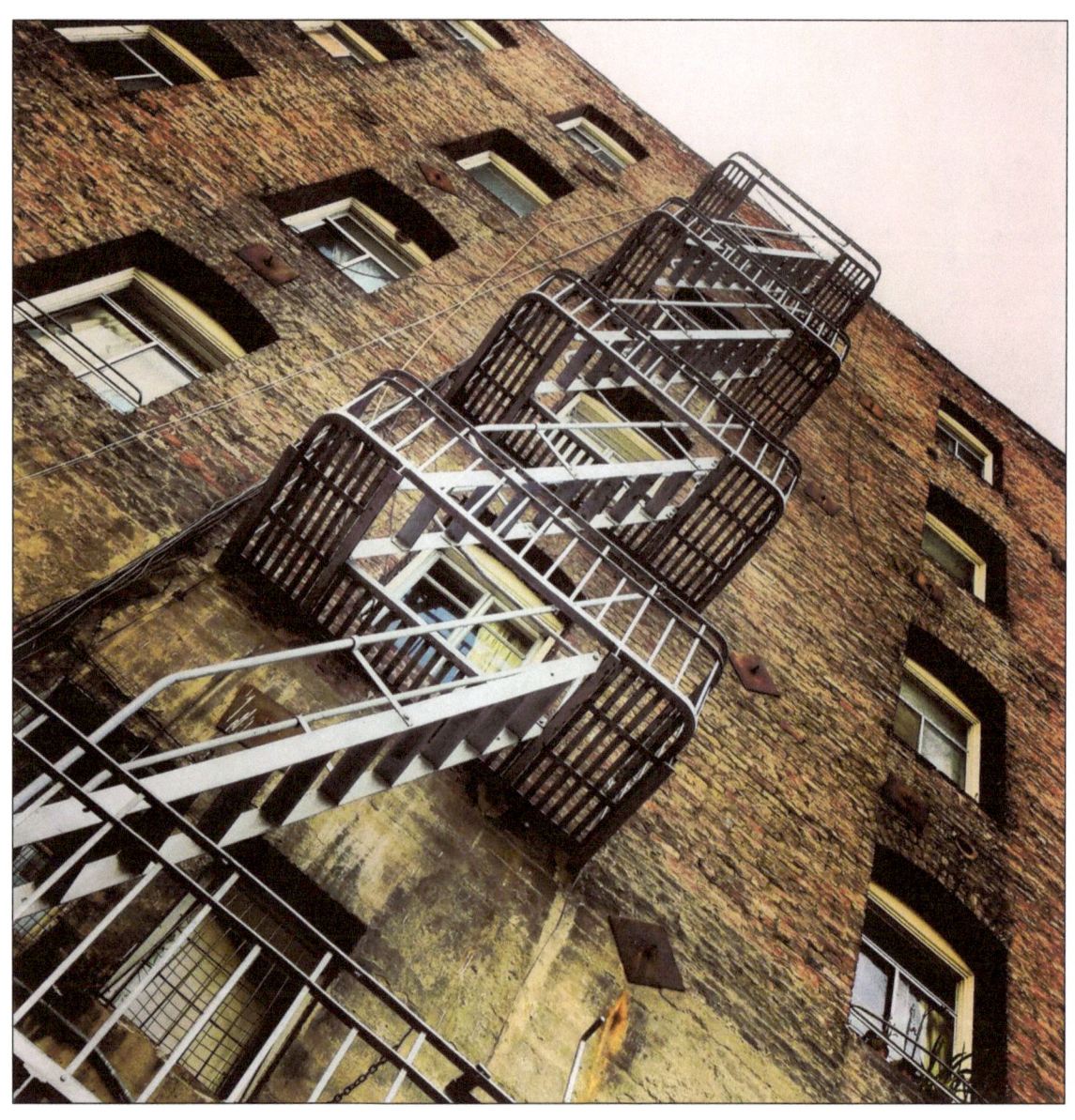

L: Old Brothel, Chinatown, San Francisco.
R: Boudin, Downtown, San Francisco.

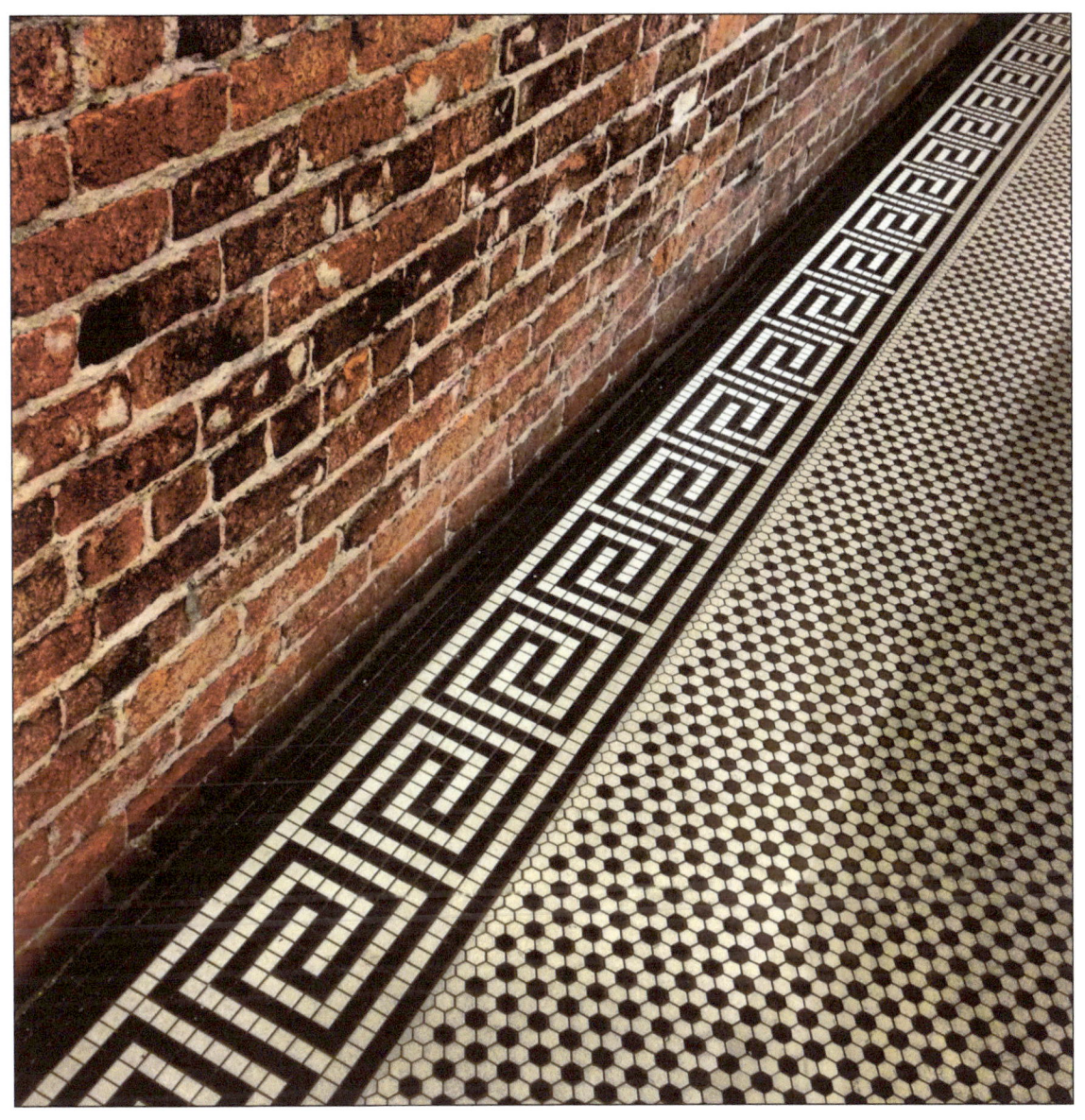

Don't compromise yourself. You are all you've got.

—Janis Joplin

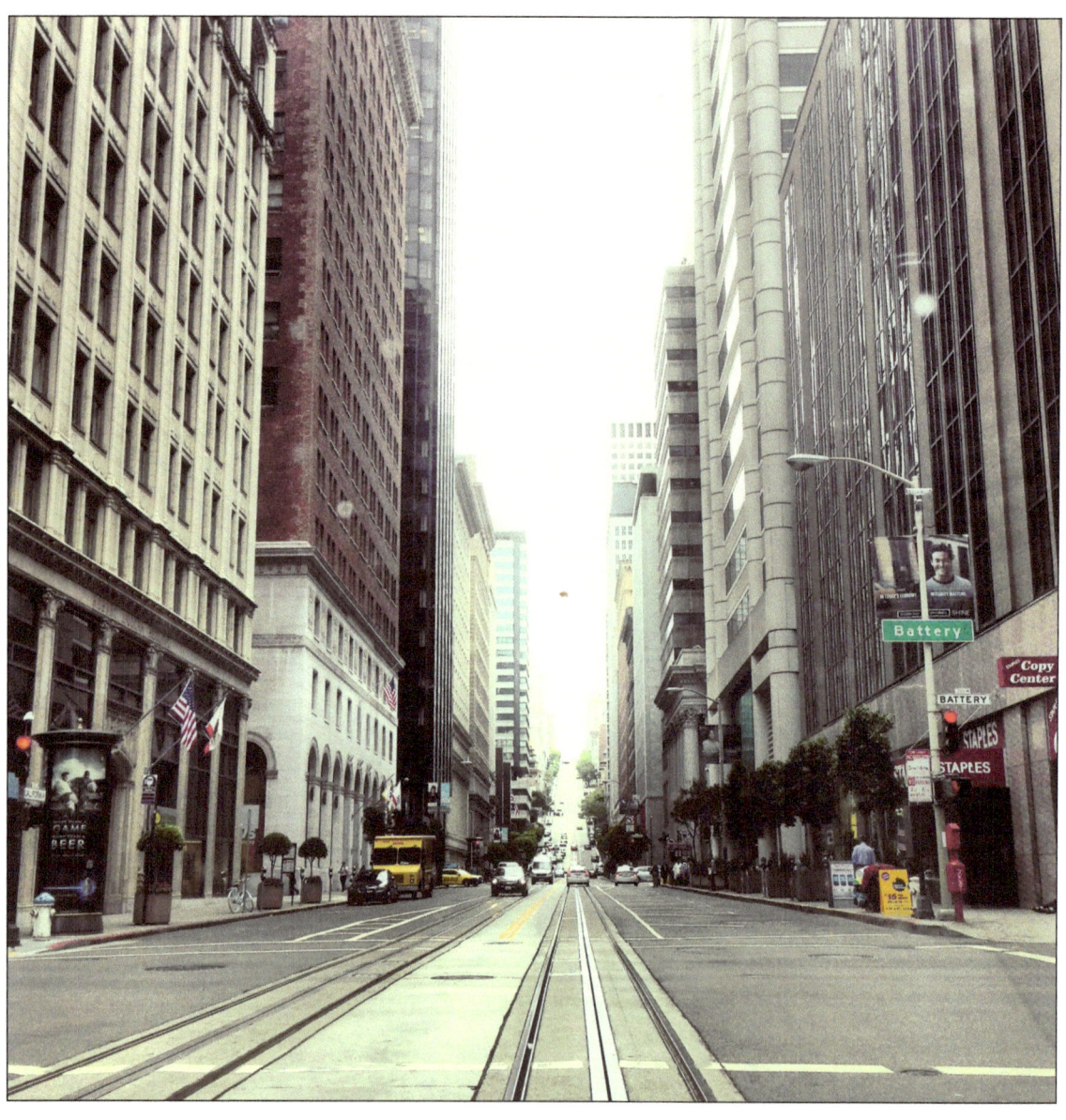

L: Outbound from financial district, San Francisco
R: Inbound to the financial district, San Francisco.

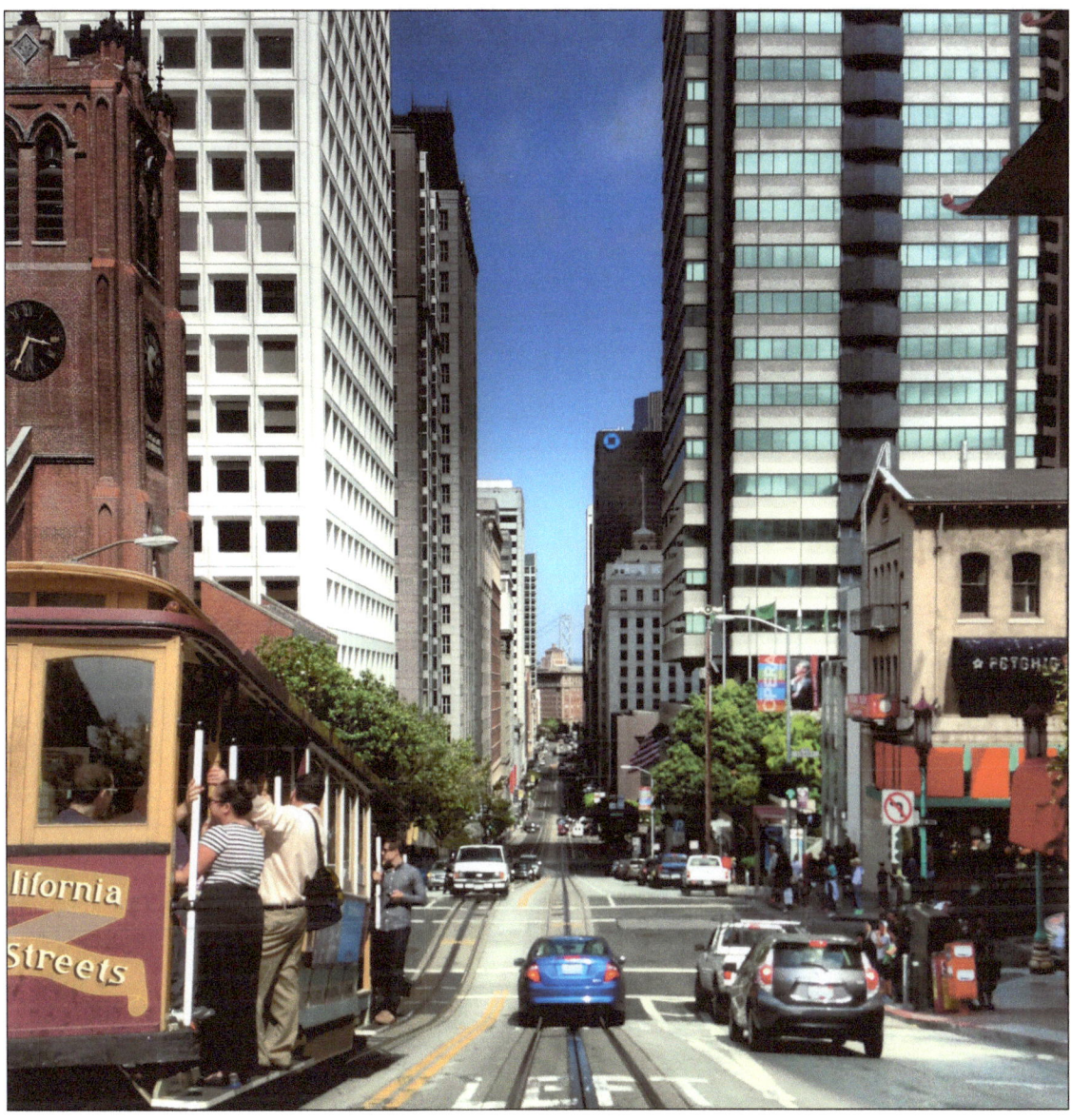

The cynicism that you have is not your real soul.

—Yoko Ono

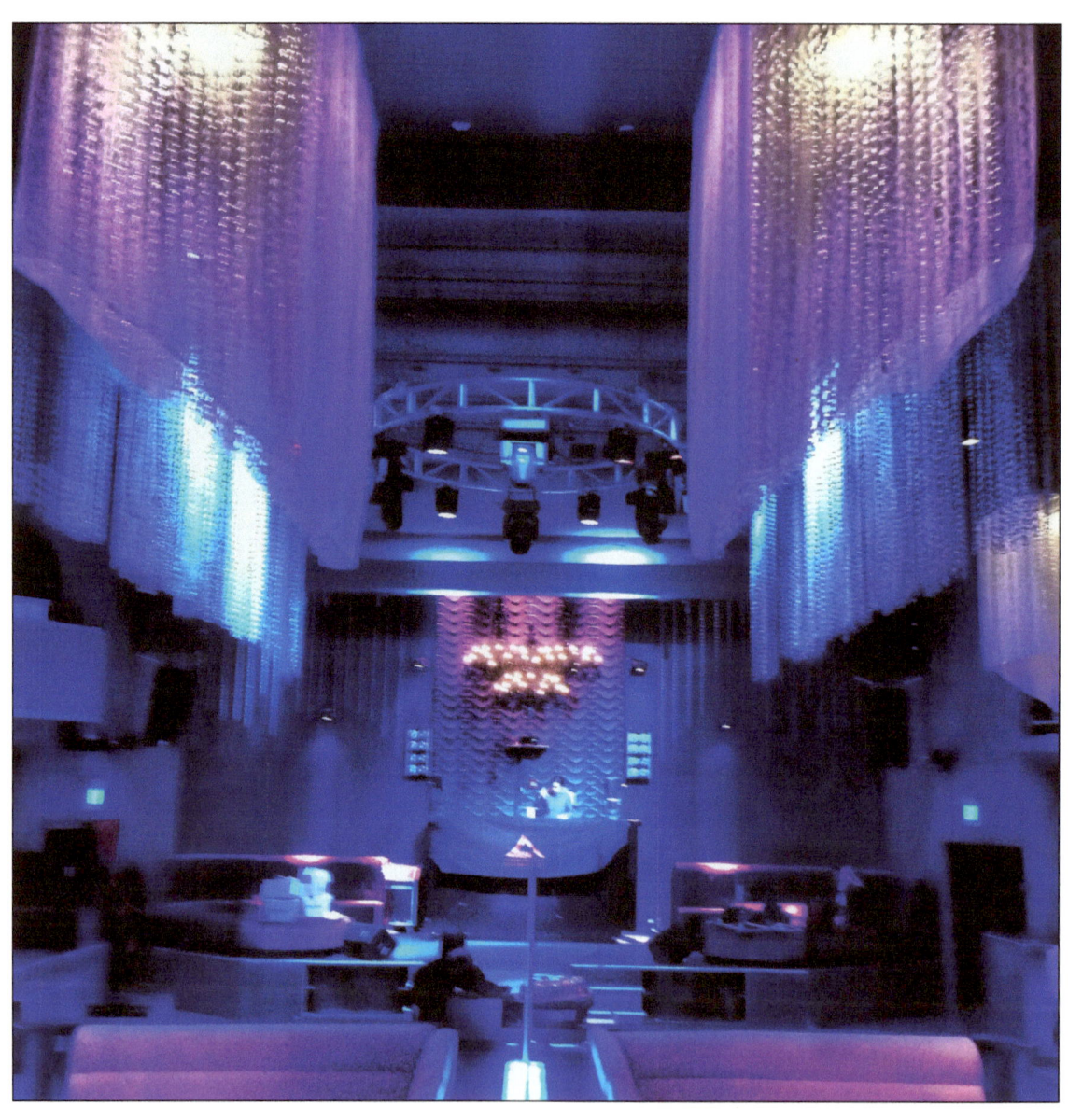

L: Pure Lounge, Silicon Valley.
R: Flying coach.

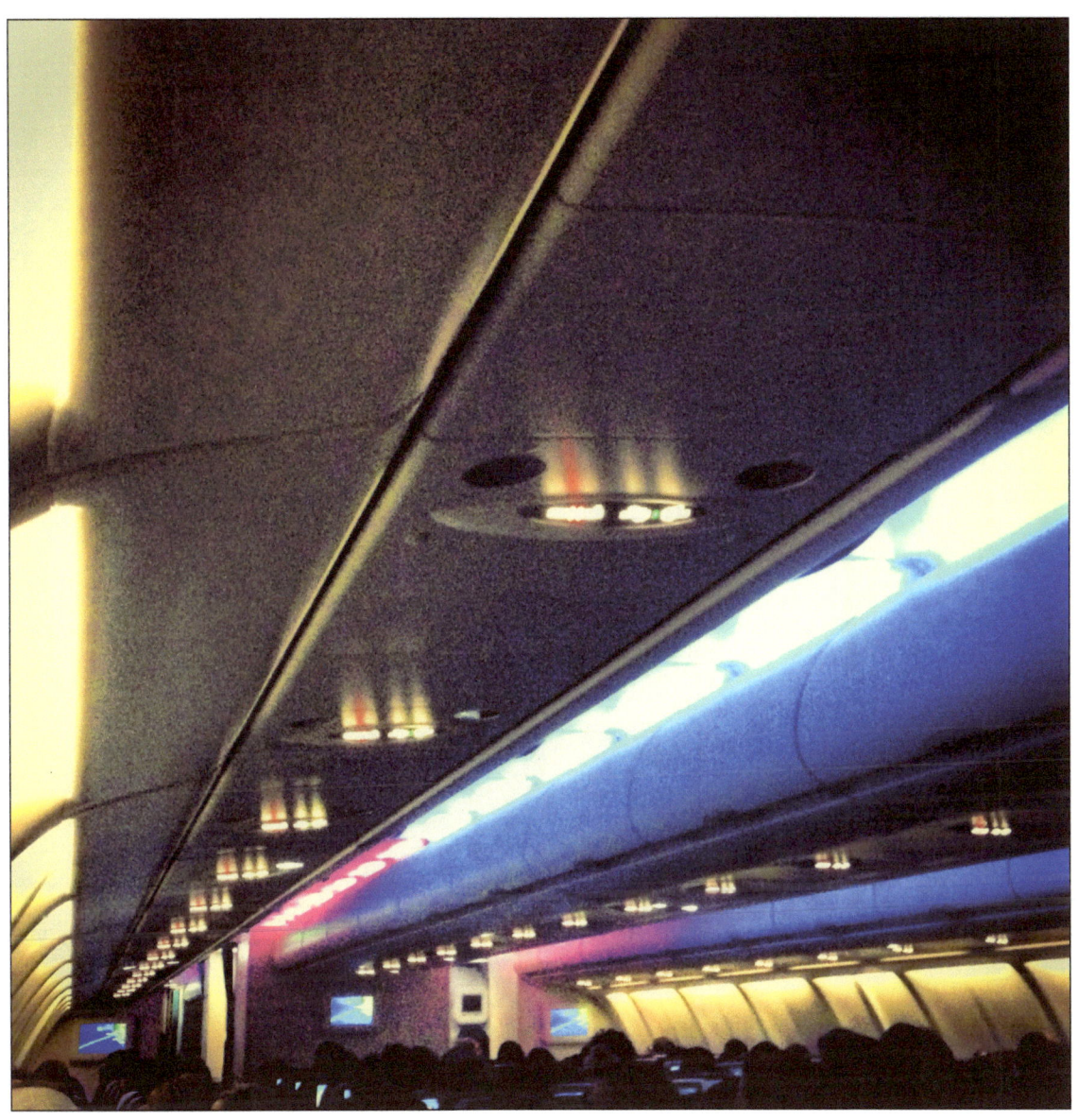

True wealth is having the knowledge to maneuver and navigate
the mental obstacles that inhibit your ability to soar.

—Rupaul

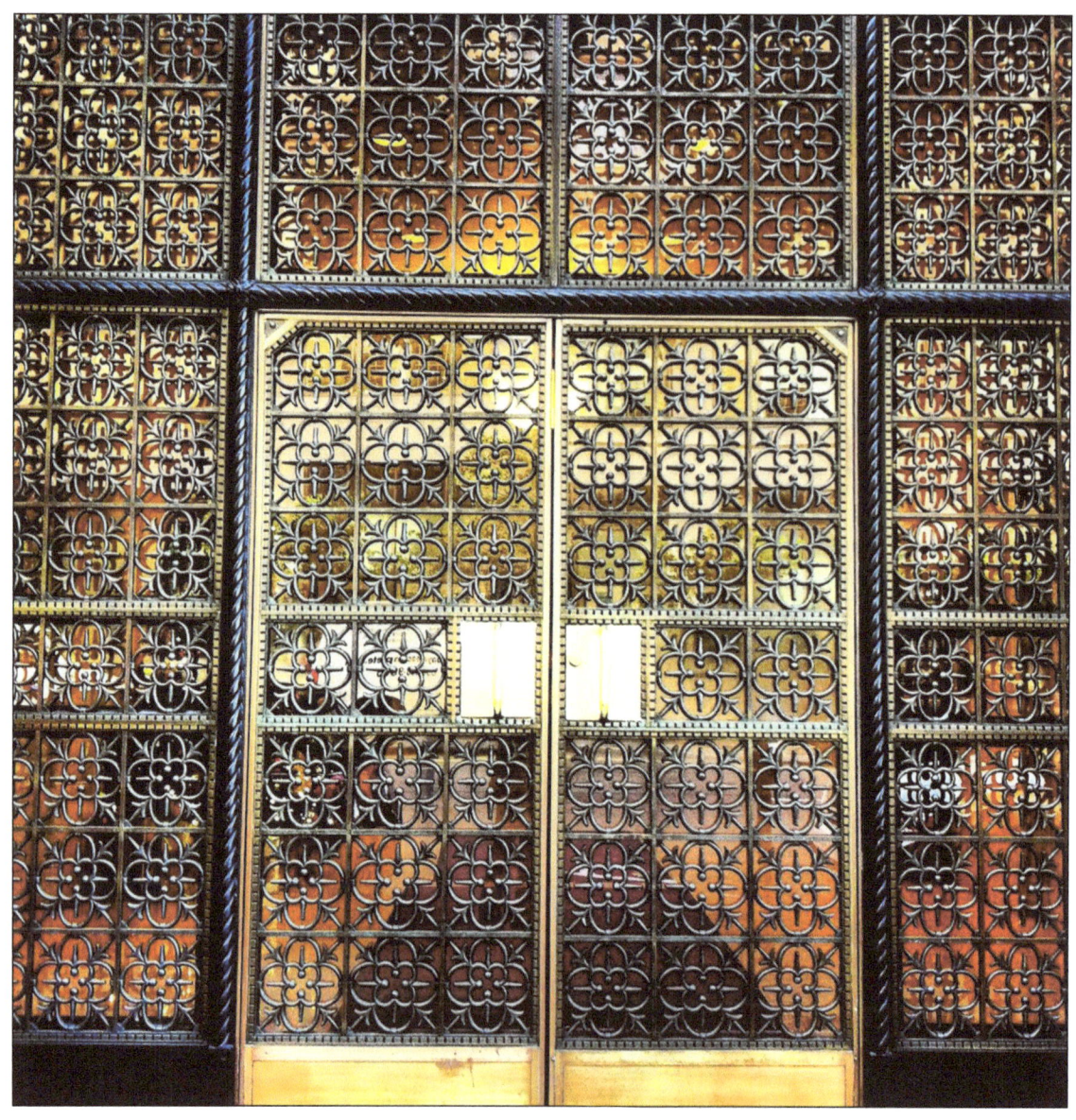

L: By Mozilla Headquarters, San Francisco.
R: Flatiron Building, San Francisco.

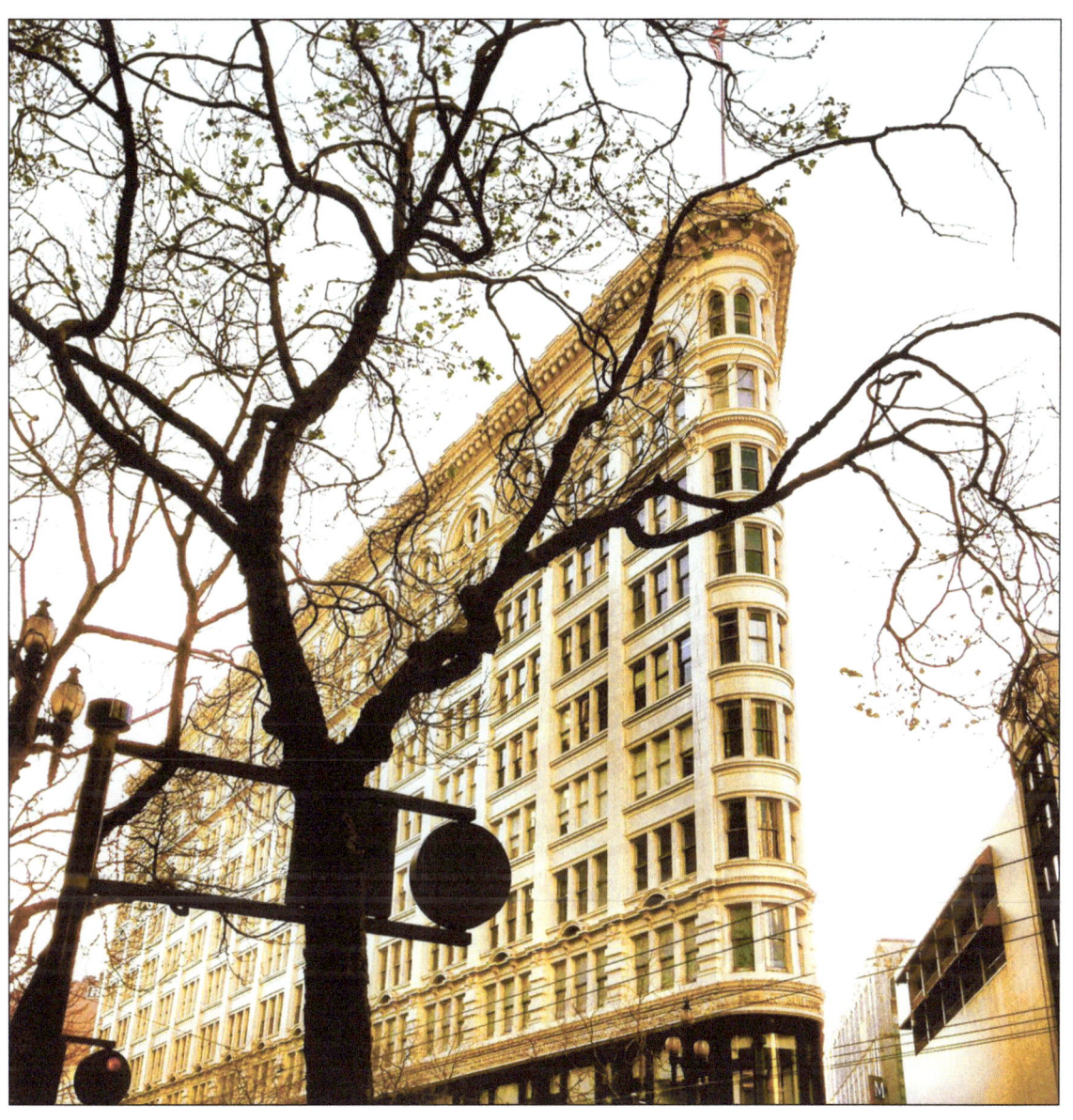

If opportunity doesn't knock, build a door.

—Milton Berle

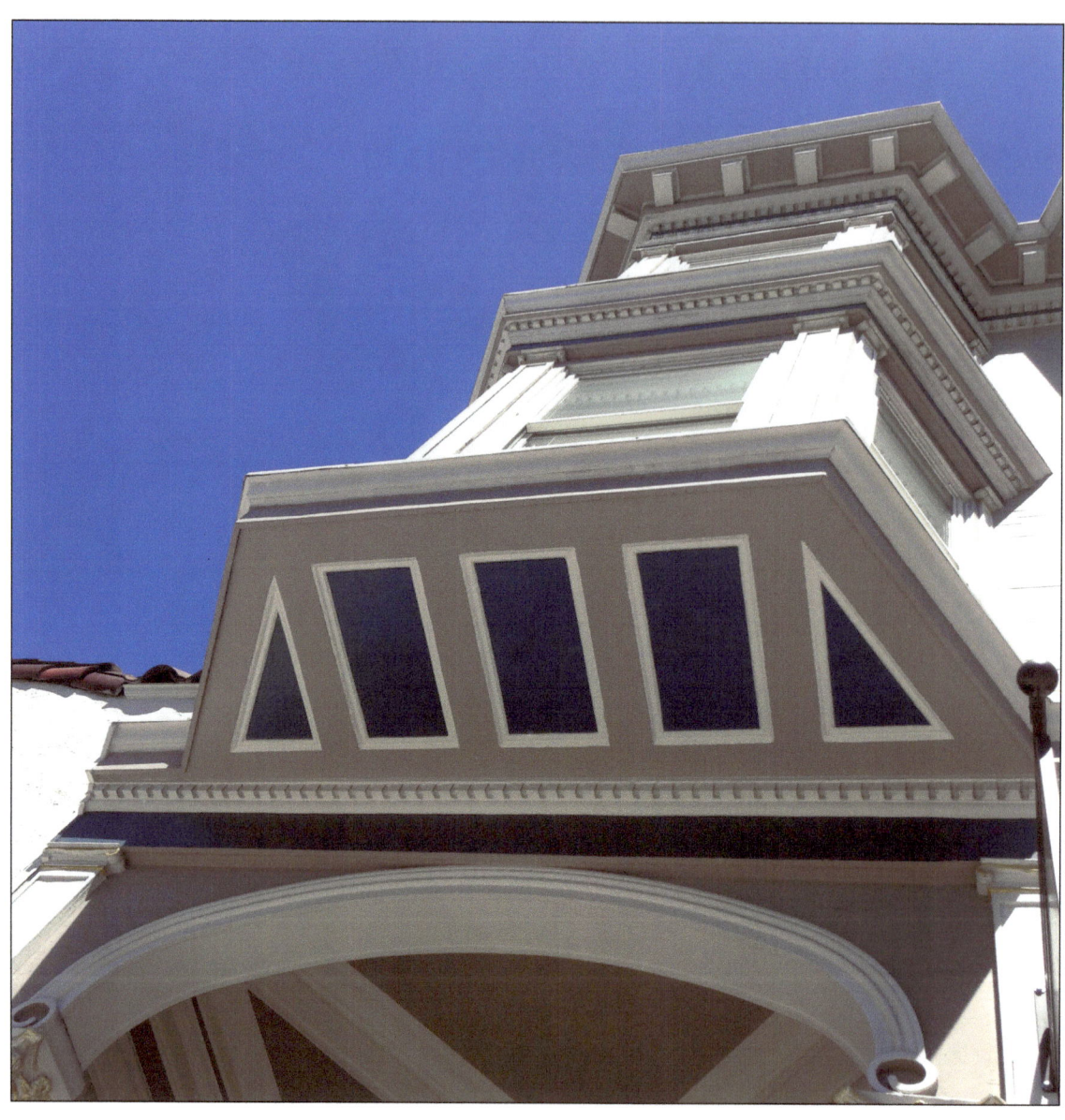

L: Hanging low on Polk Street, San Francisco.
R: High atop near Union Square, San Francisco.

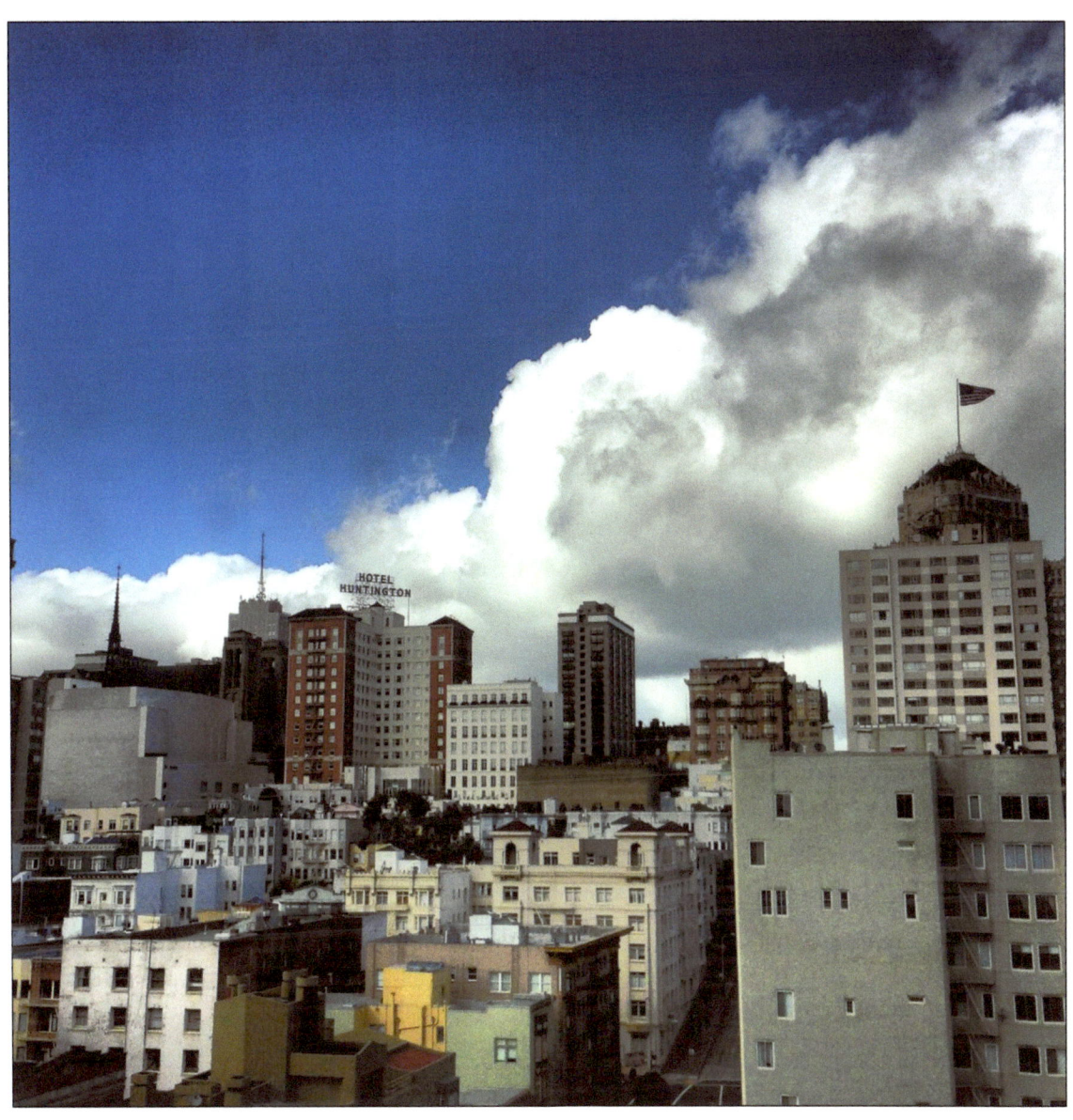

Love yourself first and everything else falls into line. You really have to love yourself to get anything done in this world.

—Lucille Ball

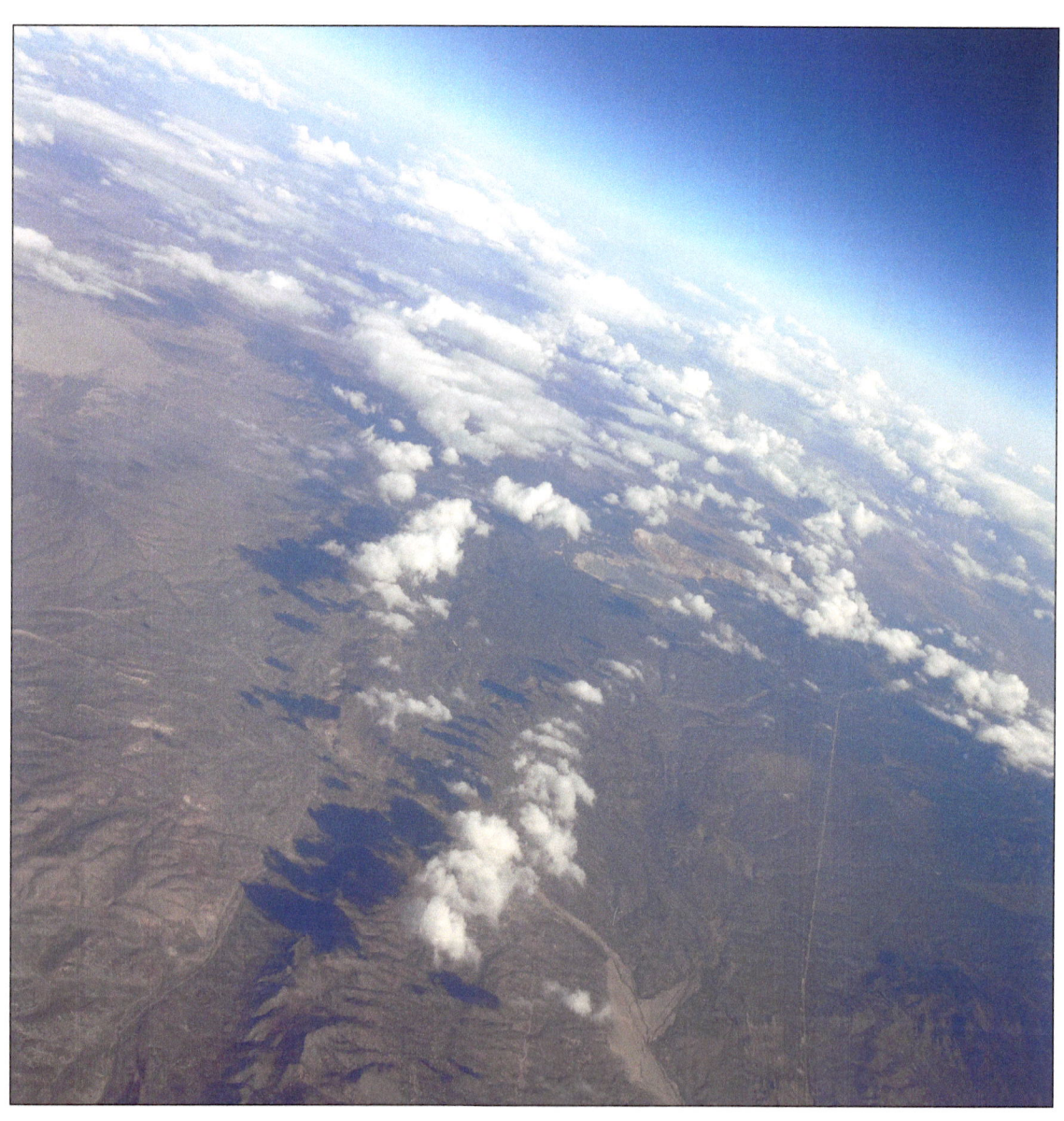

L & R: In the sky or on the ground, look up.

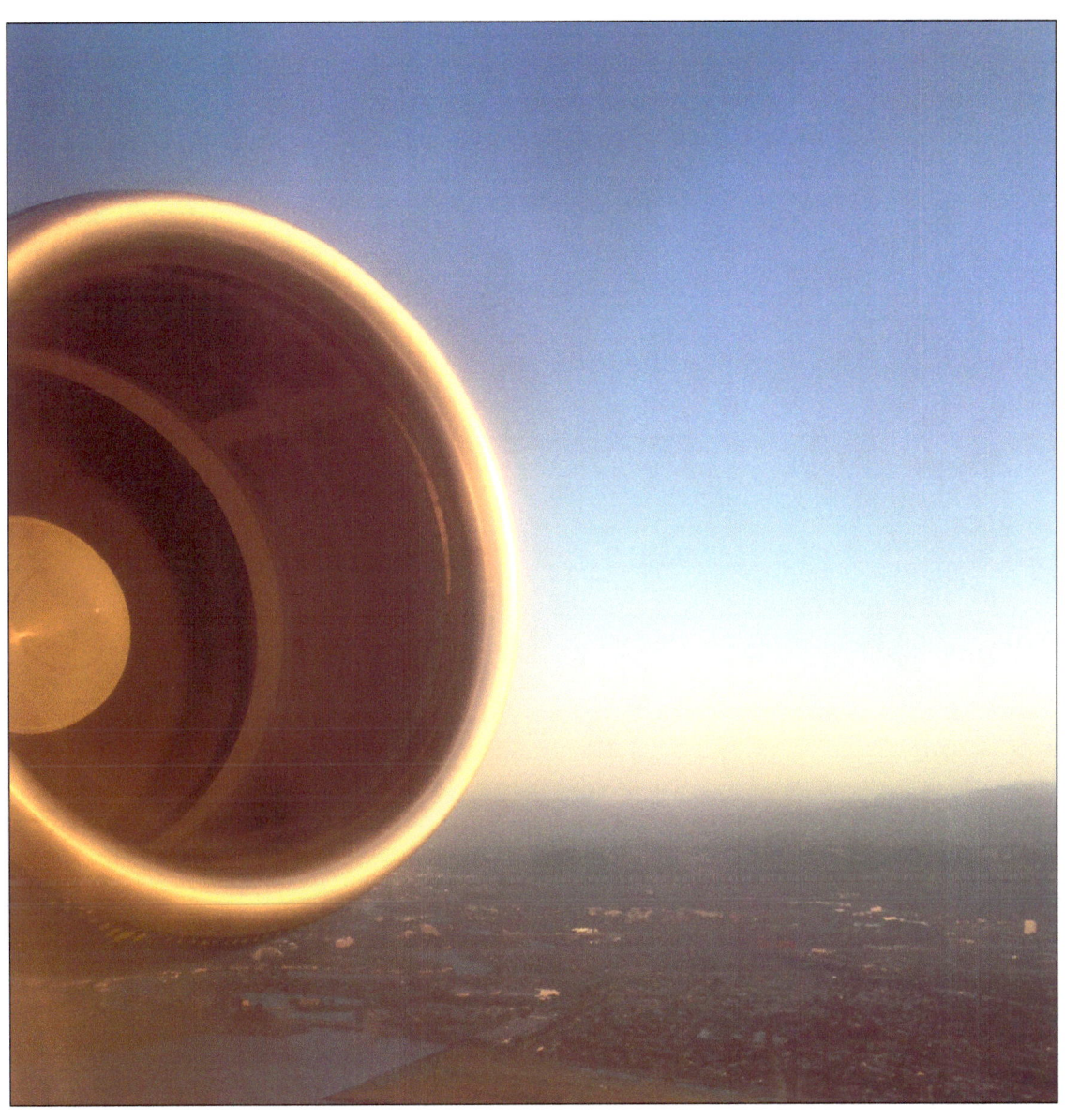

I've learned that people will forget what you said, people will forget what you did, but people will never forget how you made them feel.

—Maya Angelou

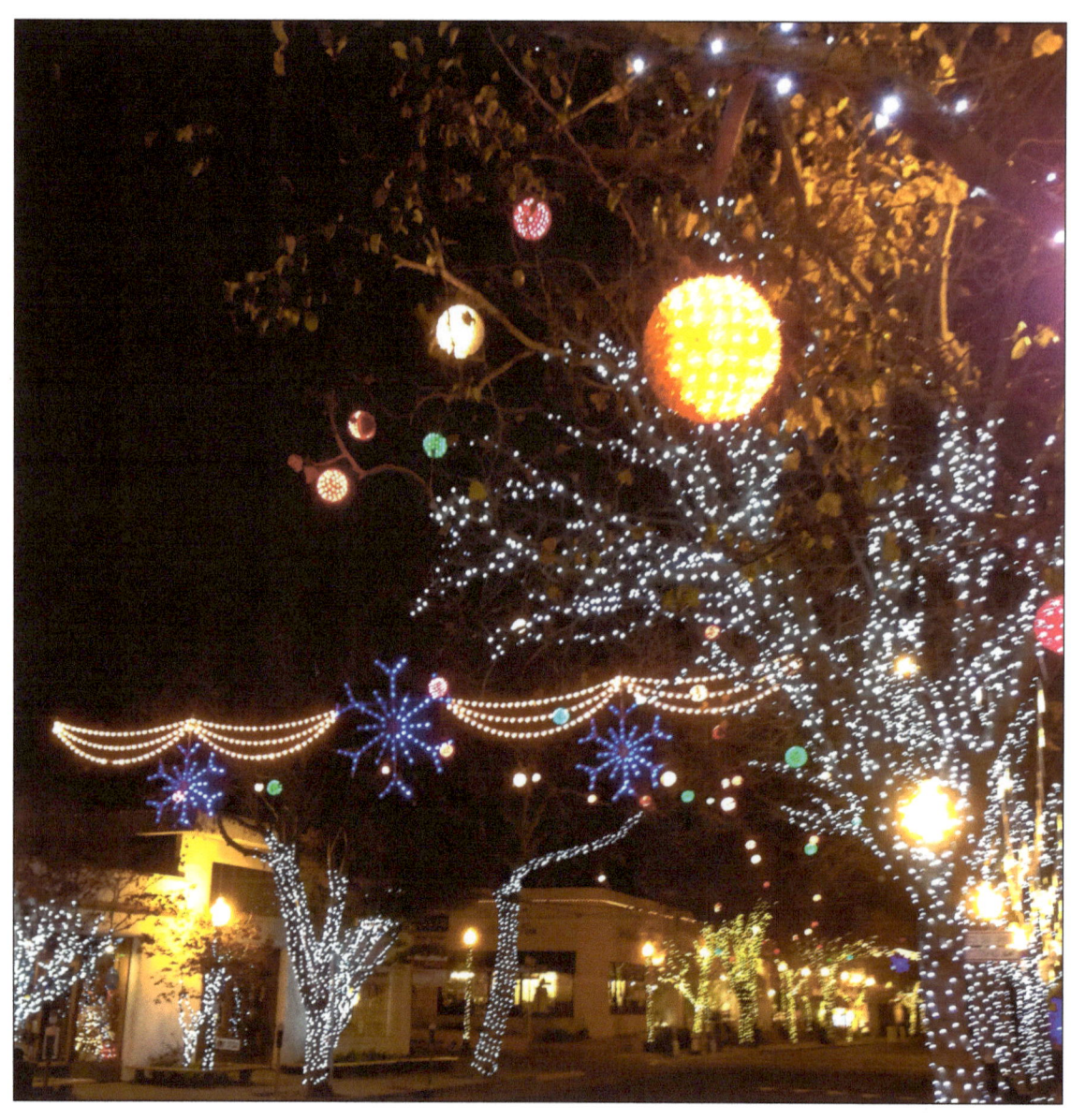

L: 4th Street, Berkeley.
R: Union Square, San Francisco.

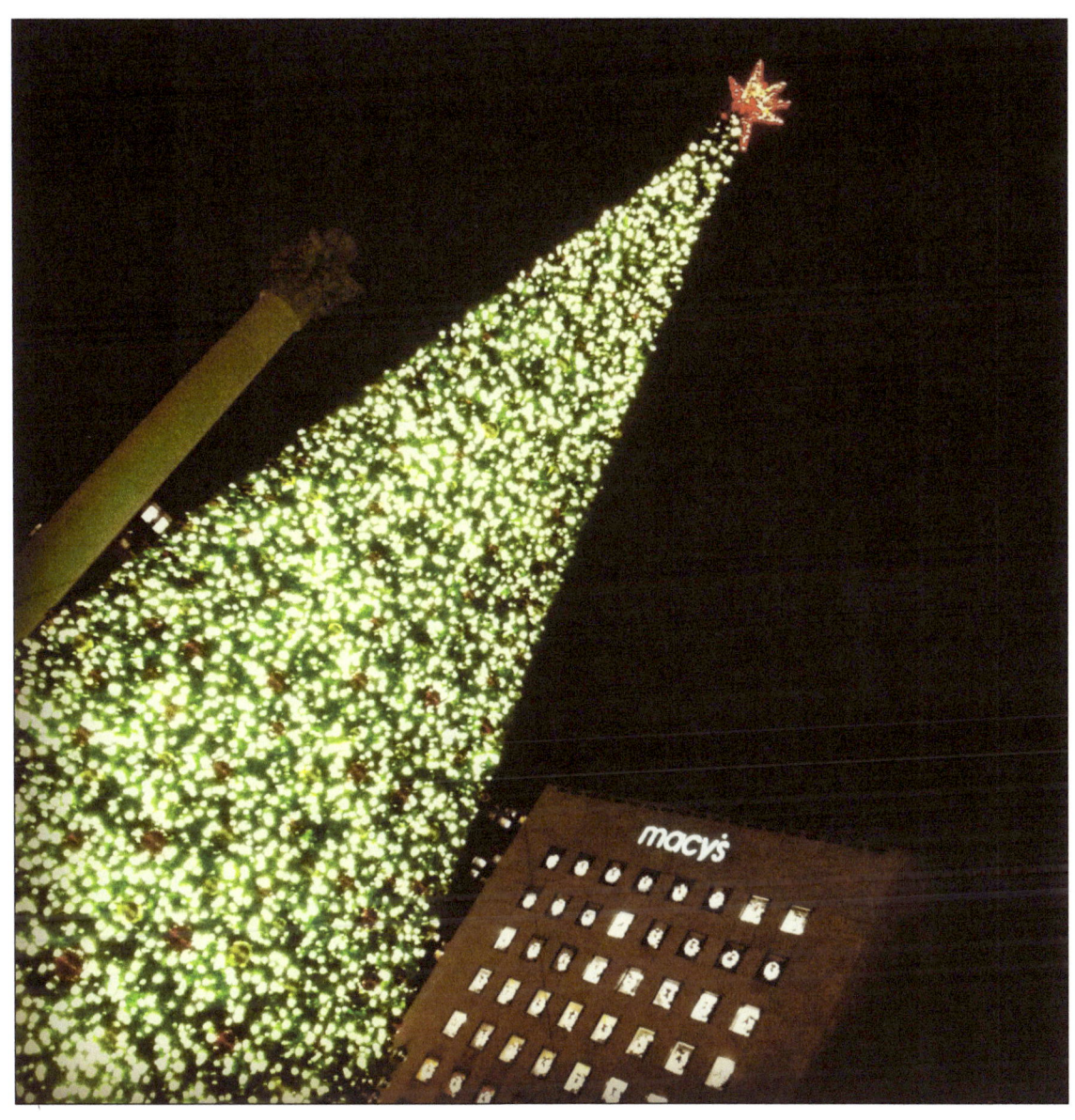

I always say shopping is cheaper than a psychiatrist.

—Tammy Faye Bakker

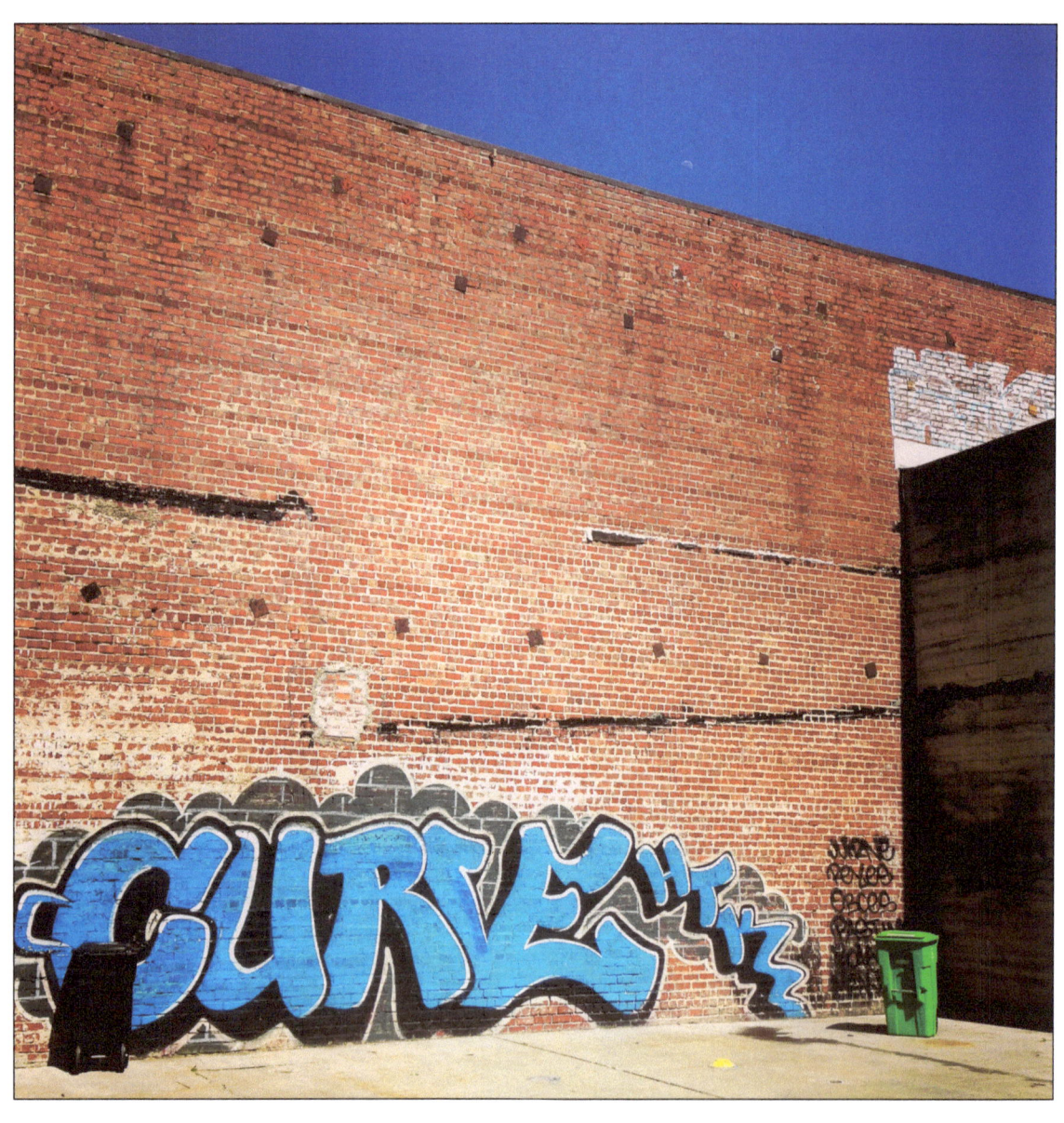

L: Back lot in Mission District, San Francisco.
(Photoshoot casting with sister)
R: Inter Continental Mark Hopkins Hotel, San Fancisco
(Featured by the San Francisco Chronicle)

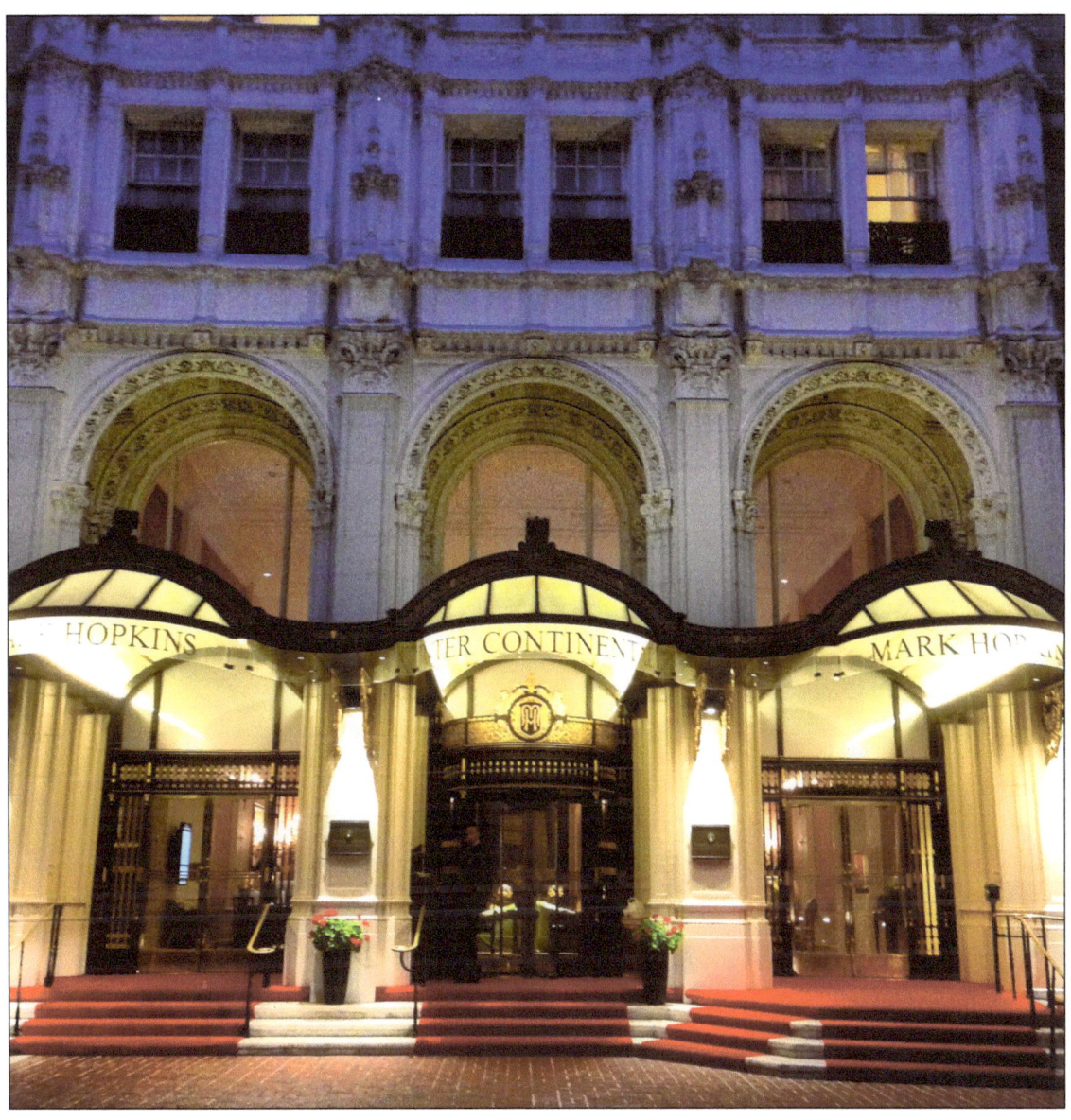

My travels led me to where I am today. Sometimes these steps have felt painful, difficult, but led to greater happiness and opportunities.

—Diana Ross

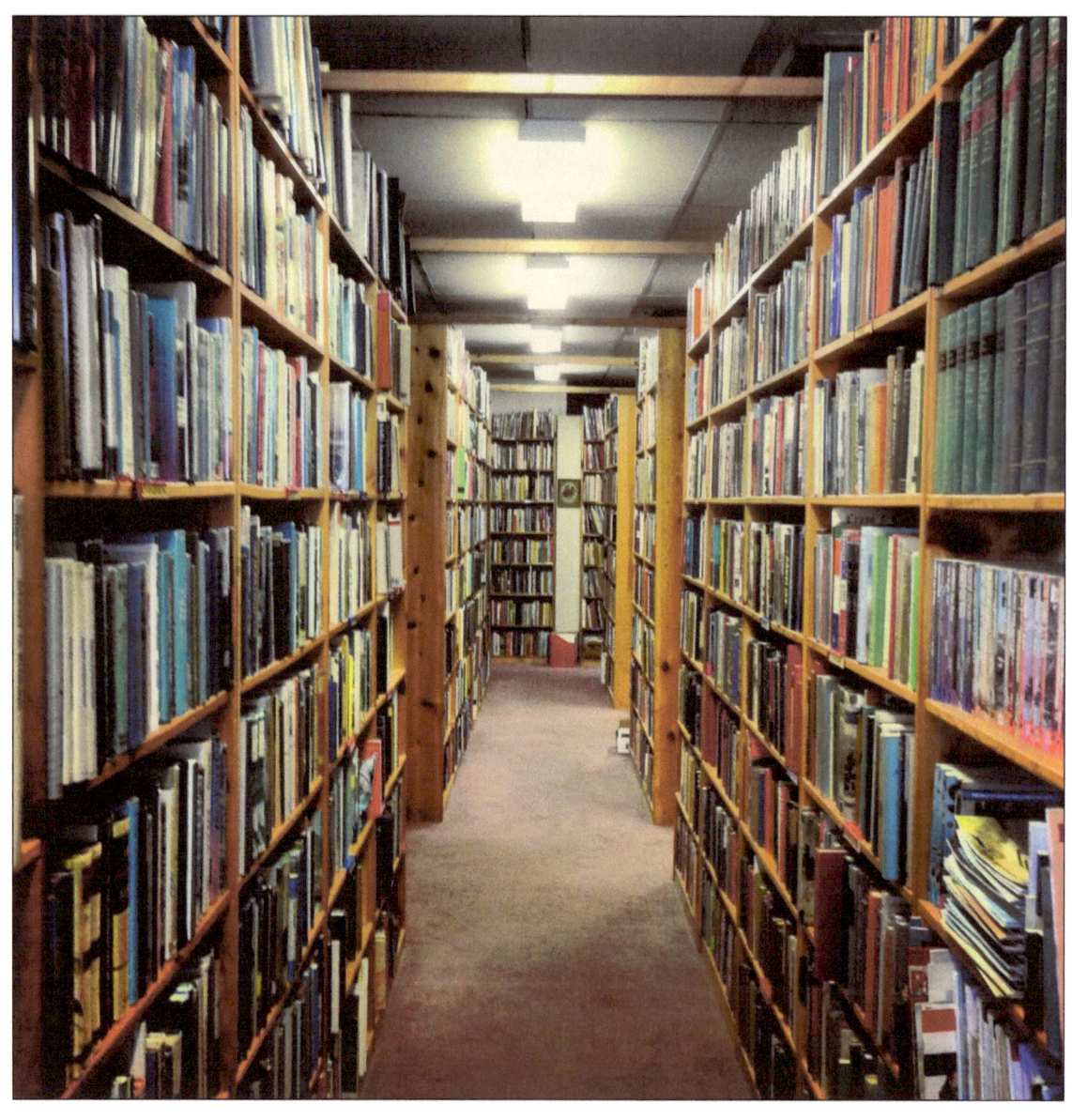

L: Bibliomania, Uptown Oakland.
R: Downtown San Francisco Alley.

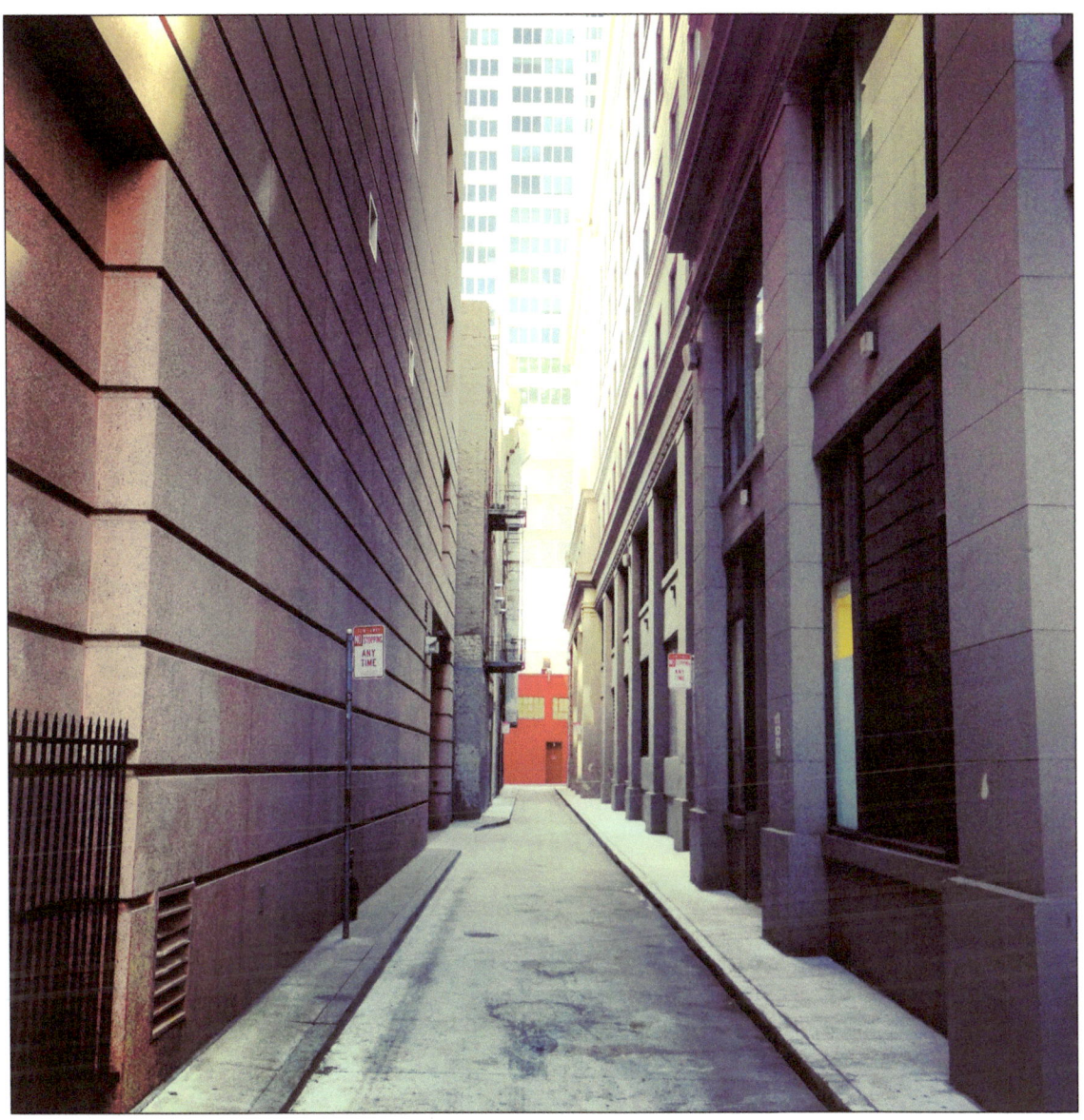

The worst enemy to creativity is self-doubt.

—Sylvia Plath

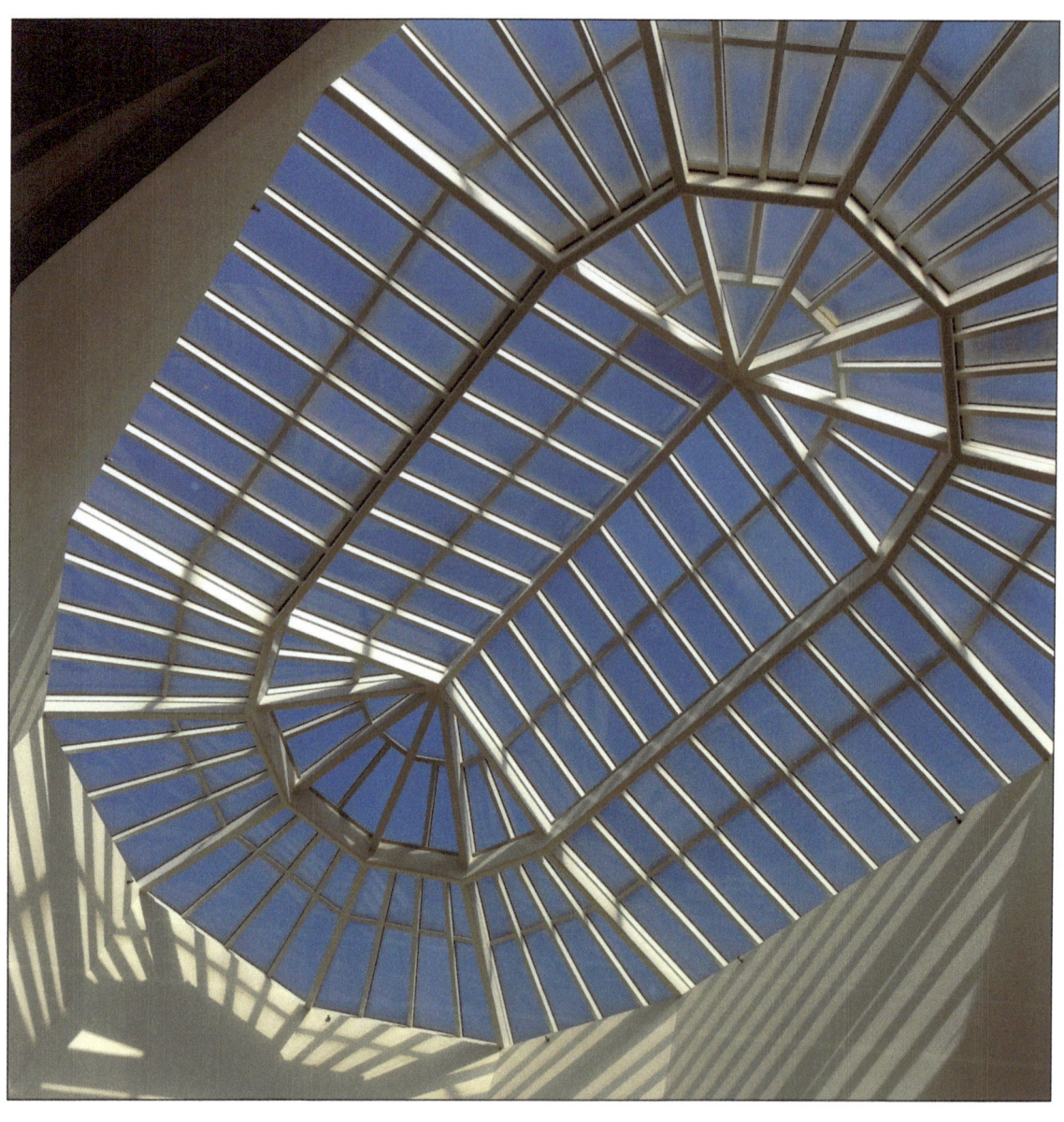

L: Barneys New York, Beverley Hills.
R: John Wayne Airport, Orange County.

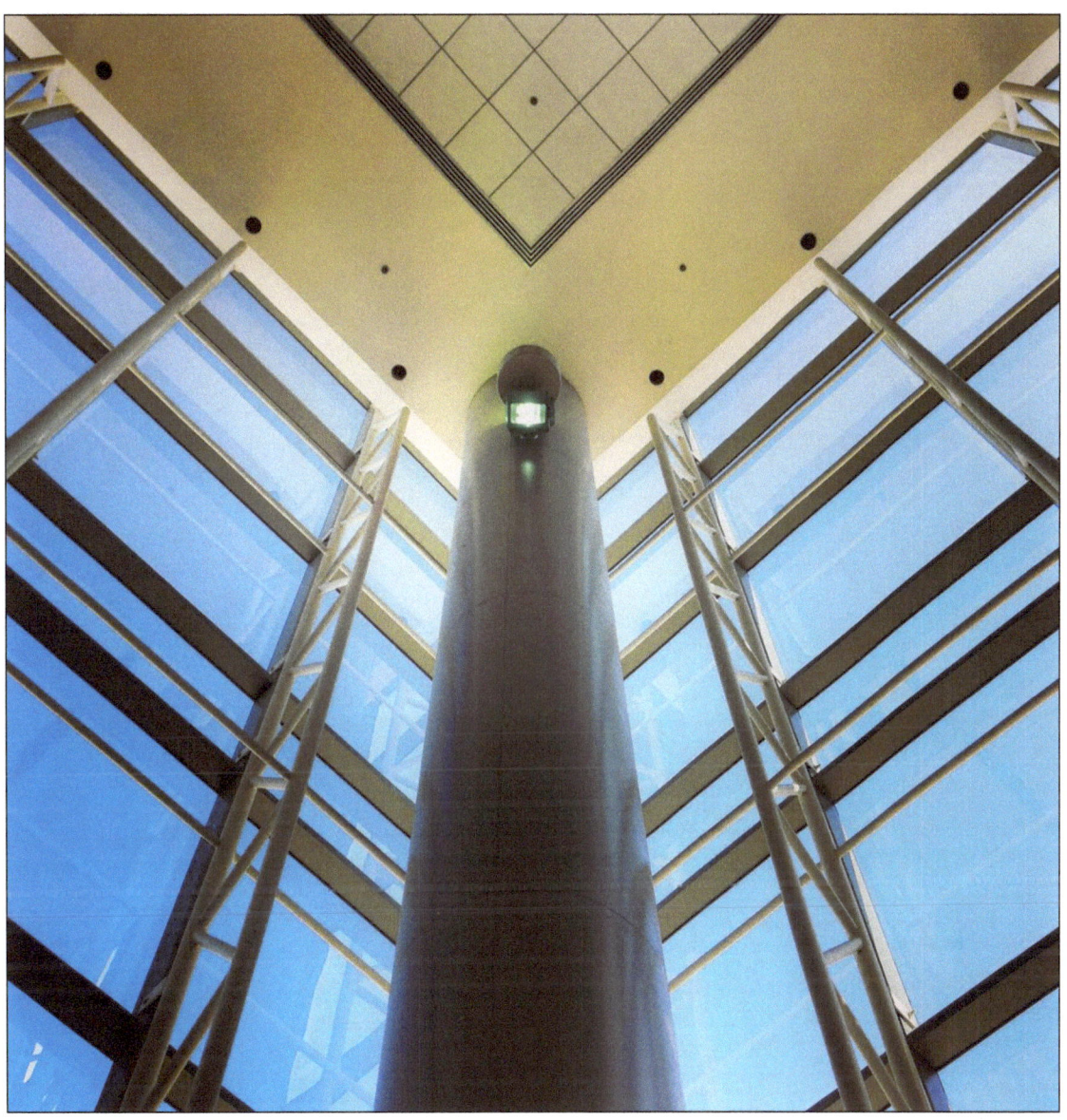

Nothing is impossible, the word itself says, "I'm possible!"

—Audrey Hepburn

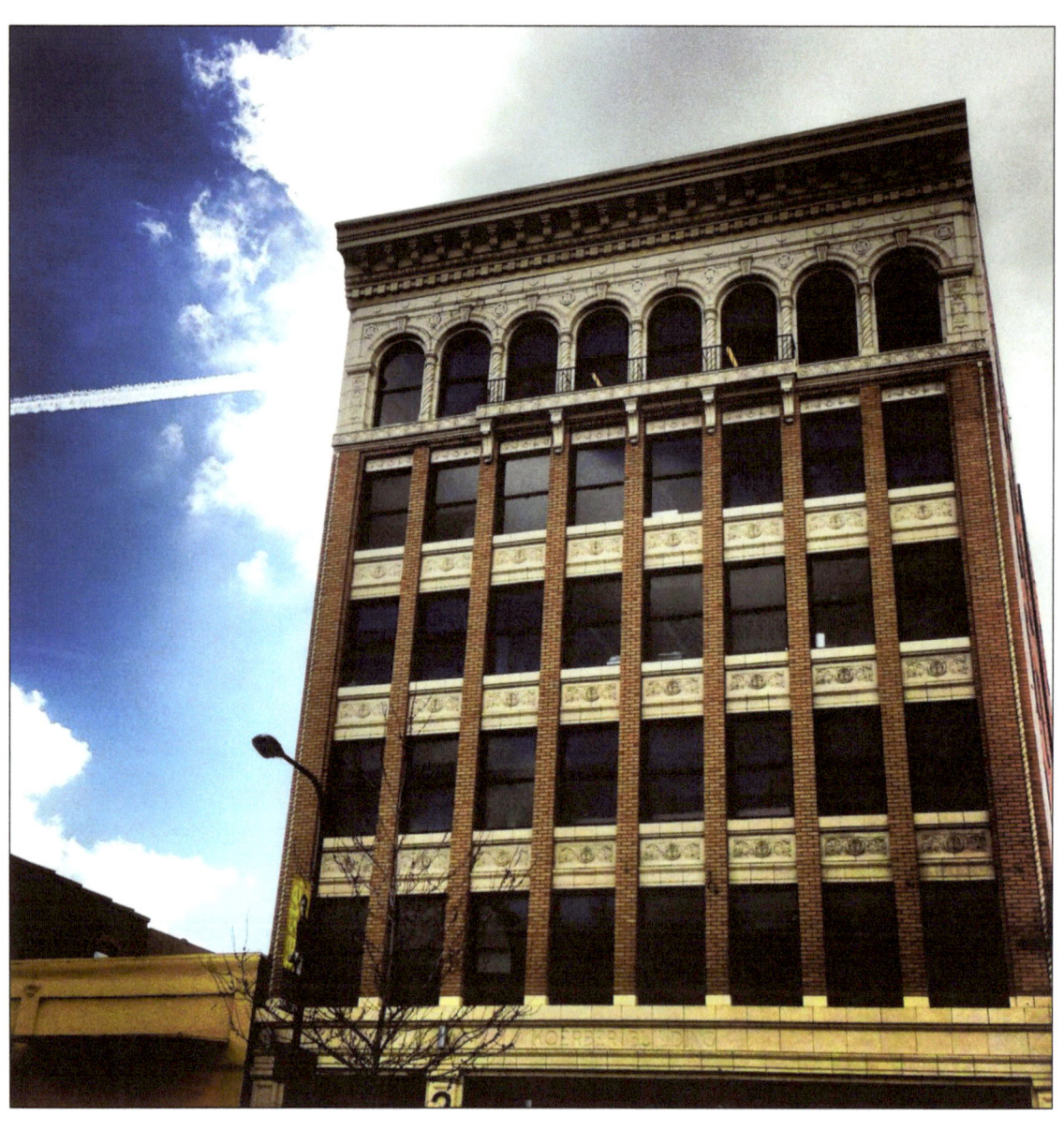

L: Lines and Angles in Berkeley
R: Hyatt Regency Waikiki

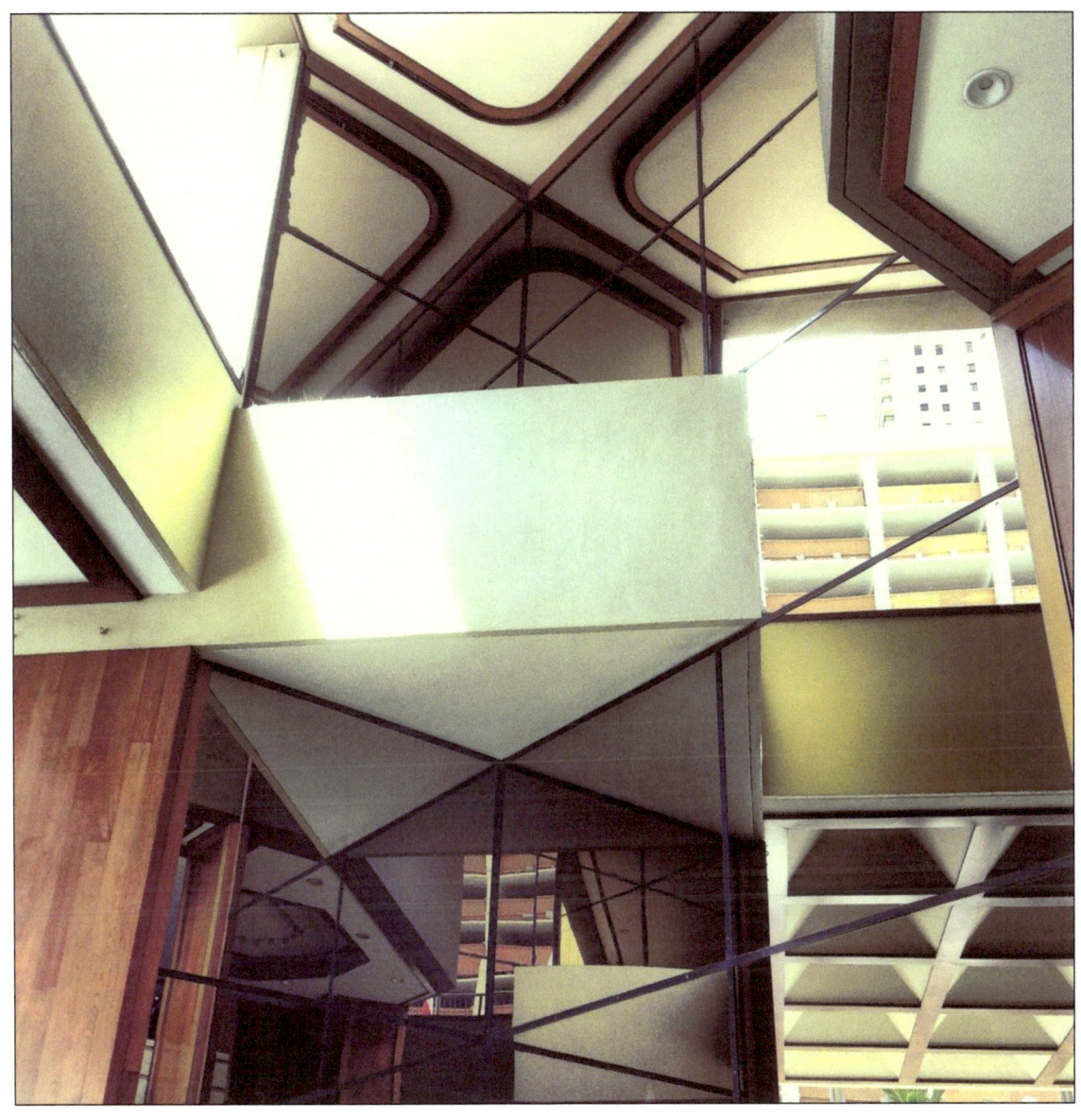

Is there anything better than to be longing for something,
when you know it is within reach?

—Greta Garbo

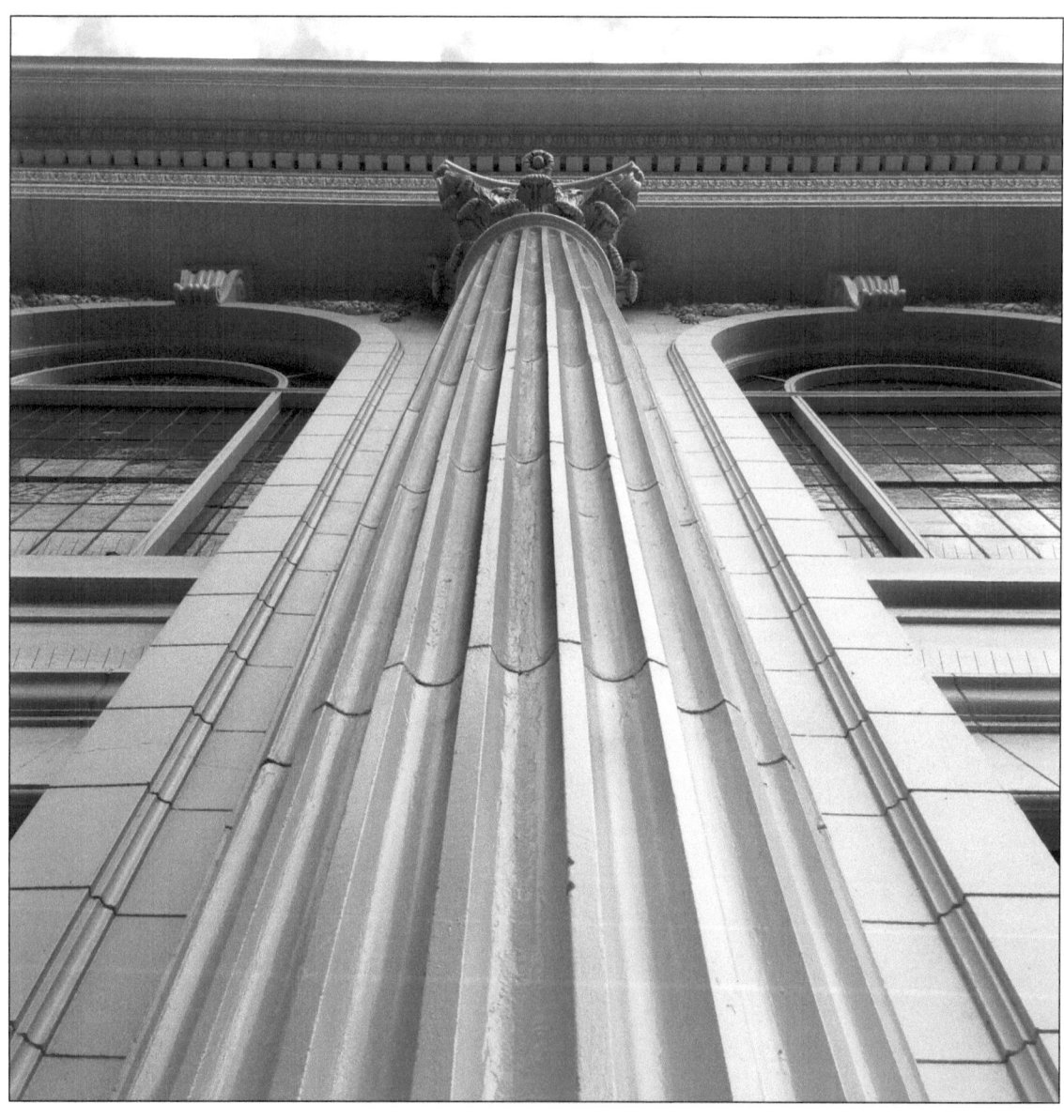

L: Academy of Art, San Francisco.
R: The Palace Hotel, San Francisco.

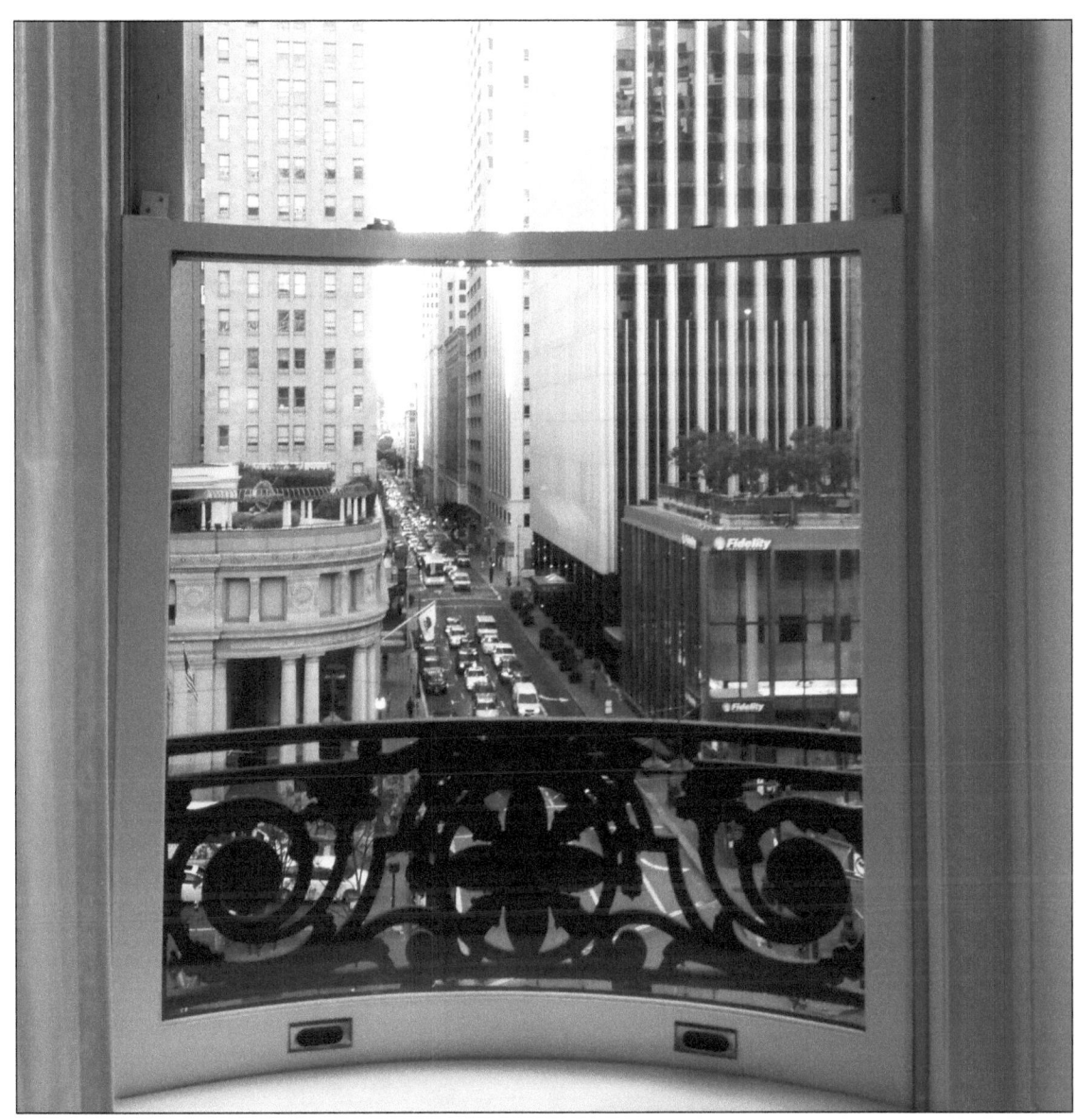

I am not a has-been. I am a will be.

—Lauren Bacall

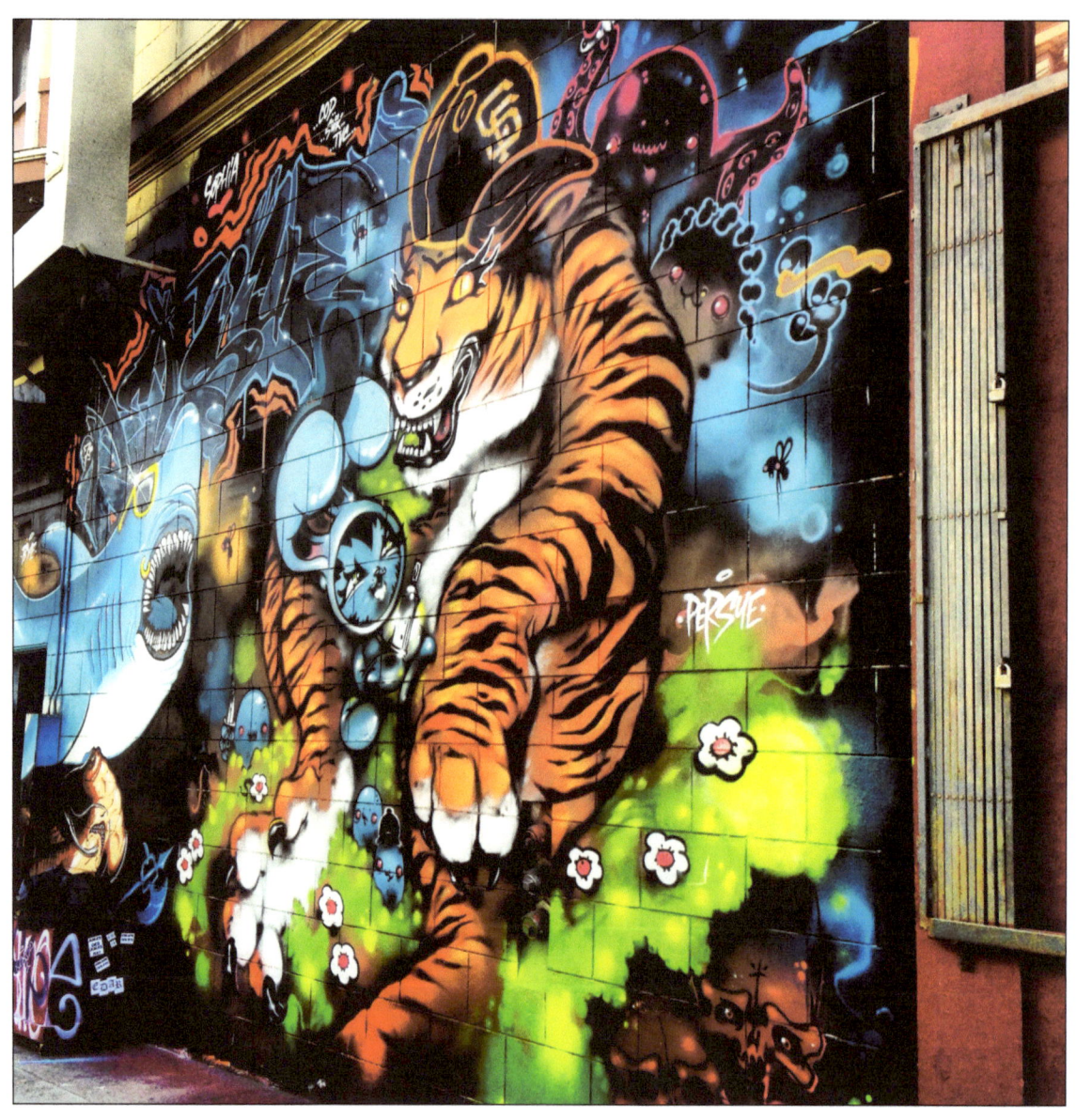

L: Street art Mission District, San Francisco.
R: San Francisco China Town against FIDI backdrop.

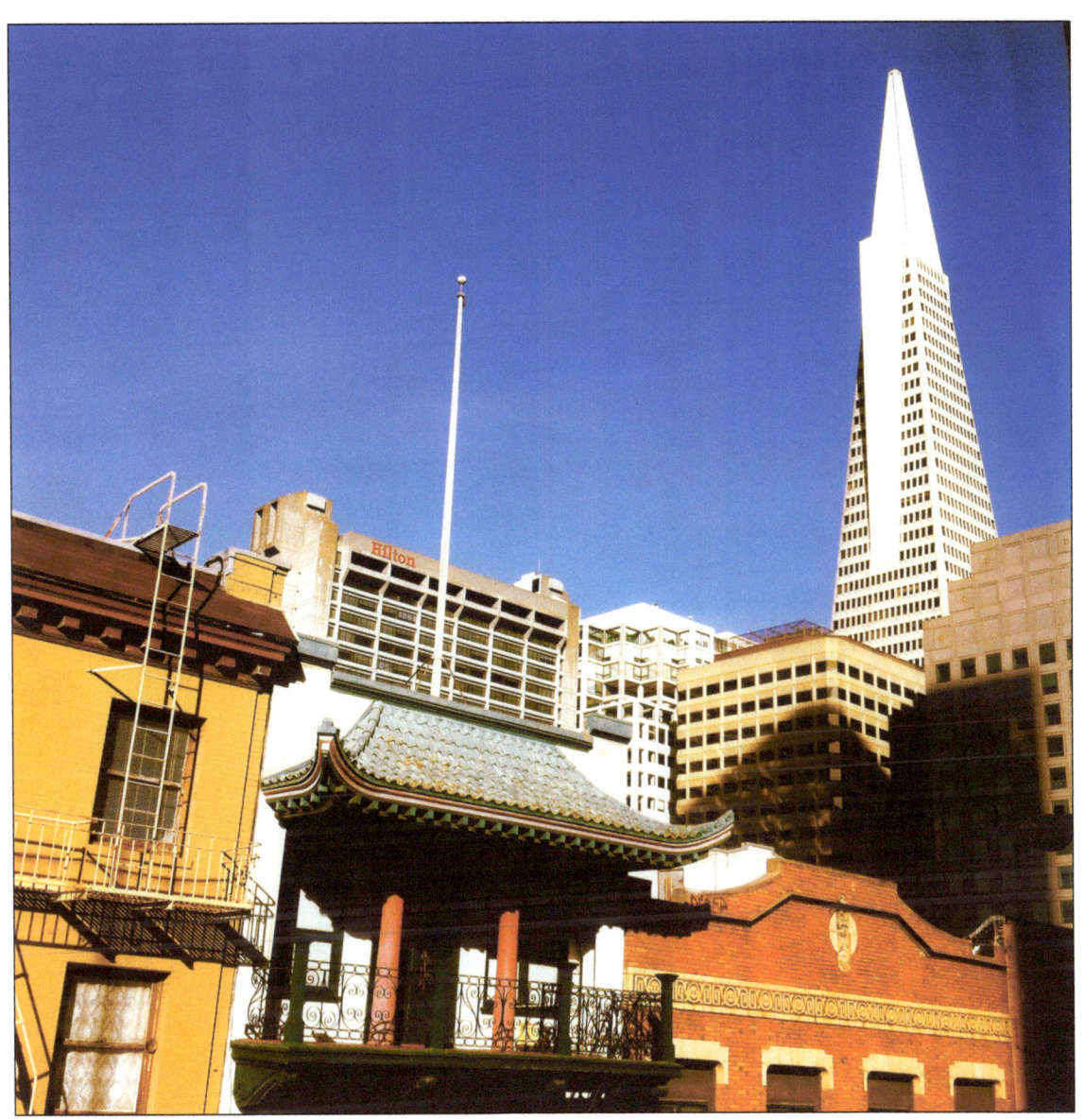

Better to live one year as a tiger, than a hundred as a sheep.

—Madonna

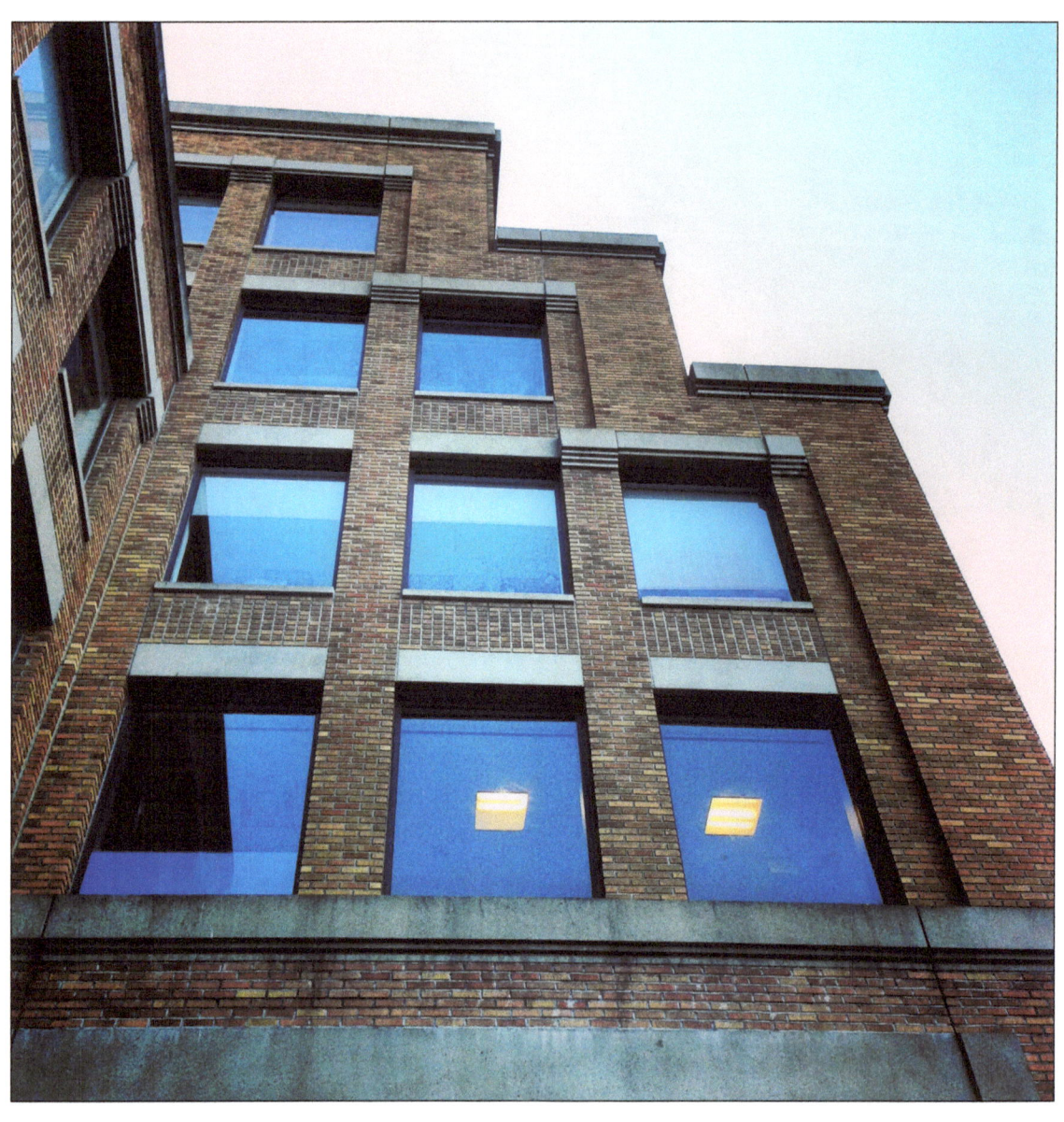

L: Palomino's Patio, San Francisco.
R: SHN Golden Gate Threatre, San Francisco.

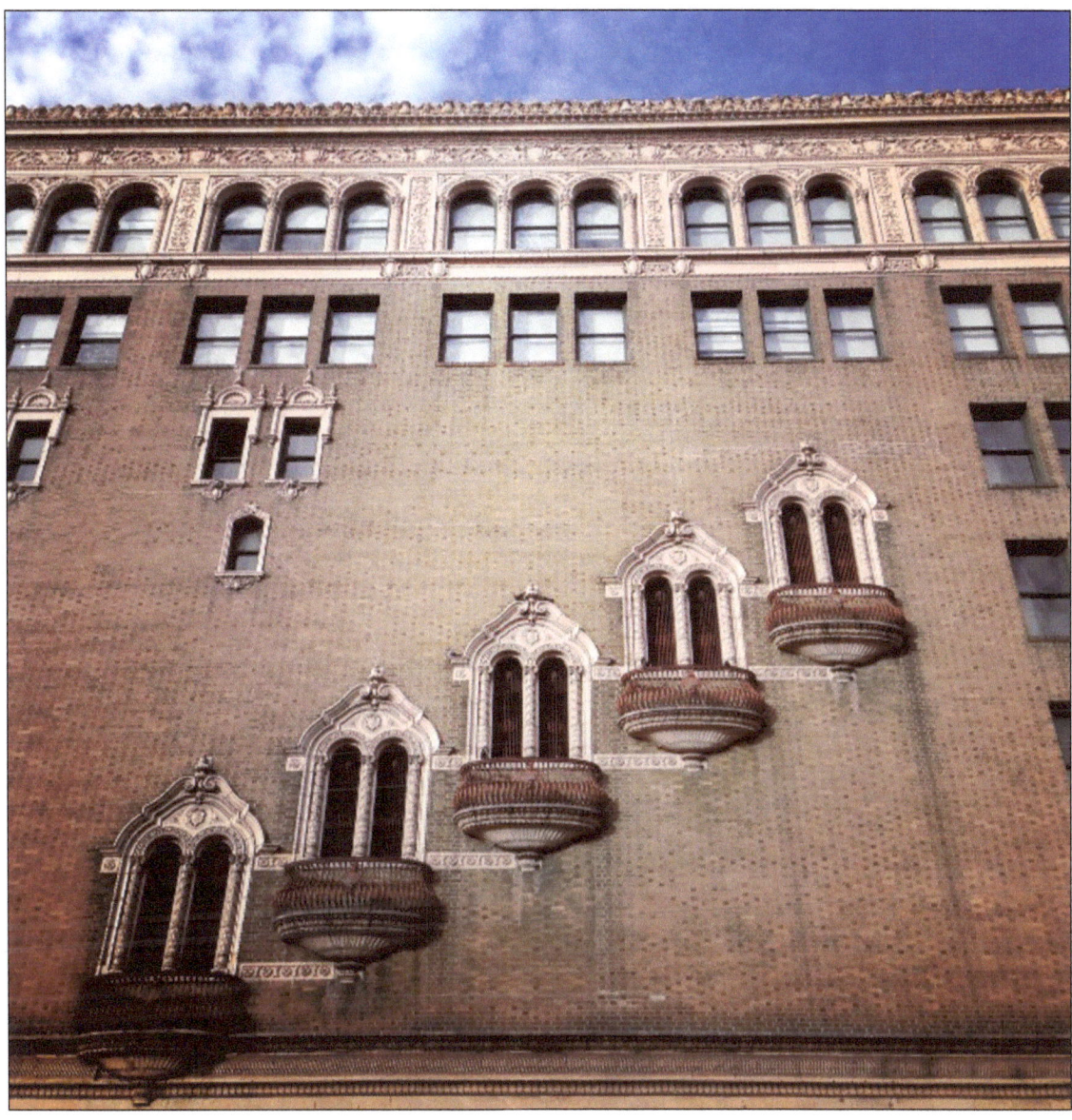

We shape our buildings; thereafter they shape us.

—Sir Winston Churchill

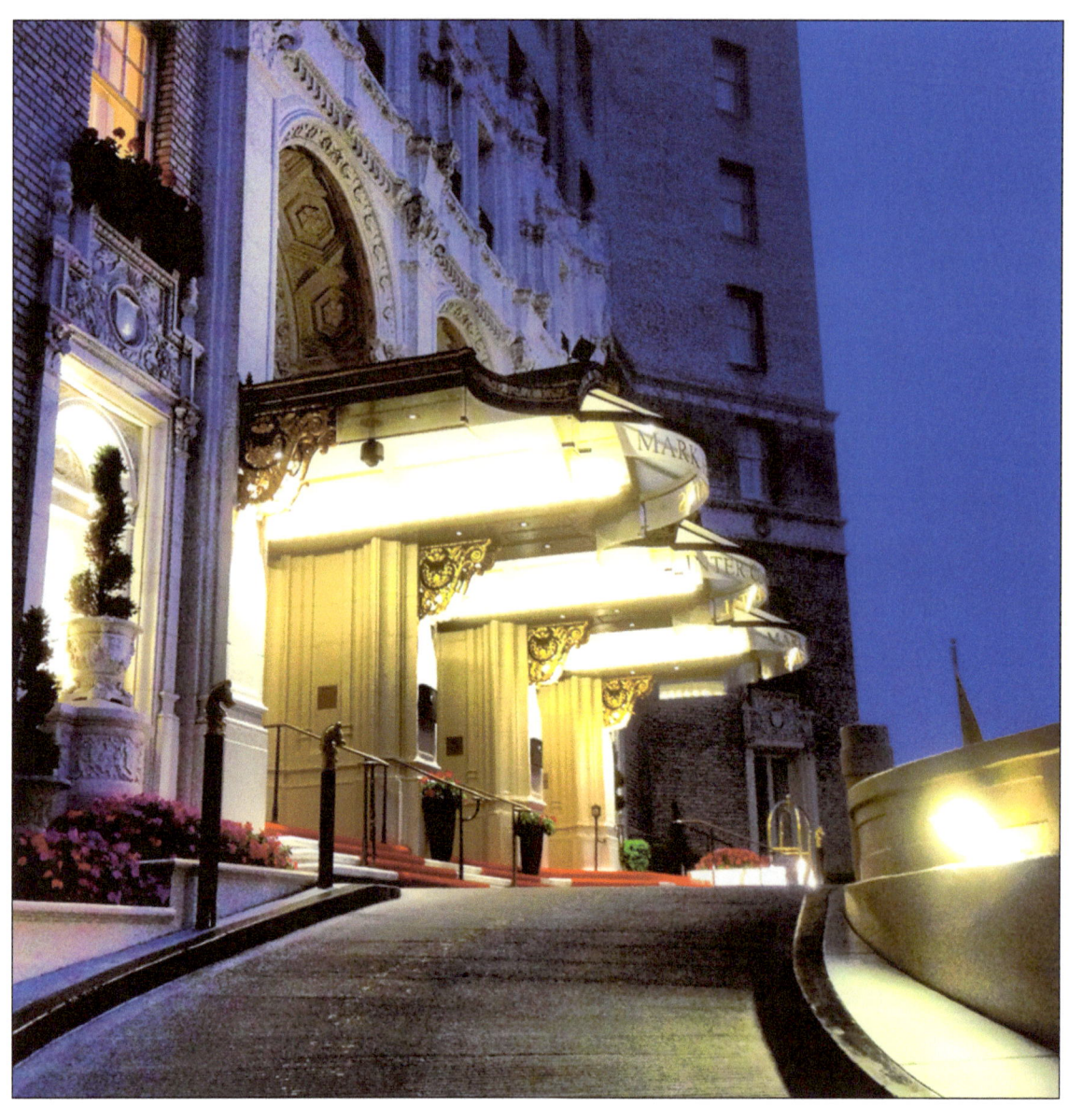

L: InterContinental Mark Hopkins, San Francisco.
R: Fairmount Hotel, San Francisco.

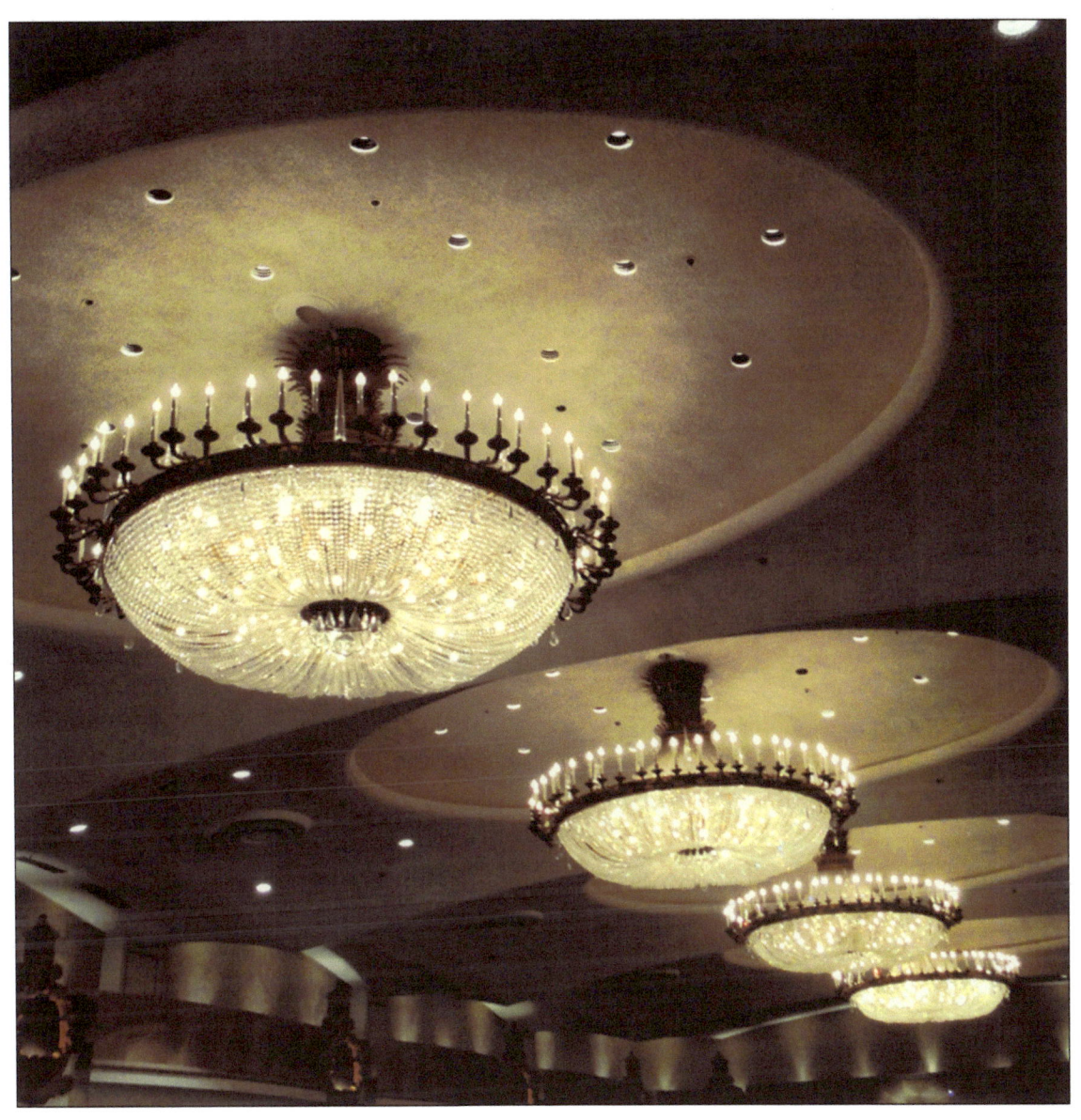

Style is knowing who you are, what you want to say,
and not giving a damn.

—Gore Vidal

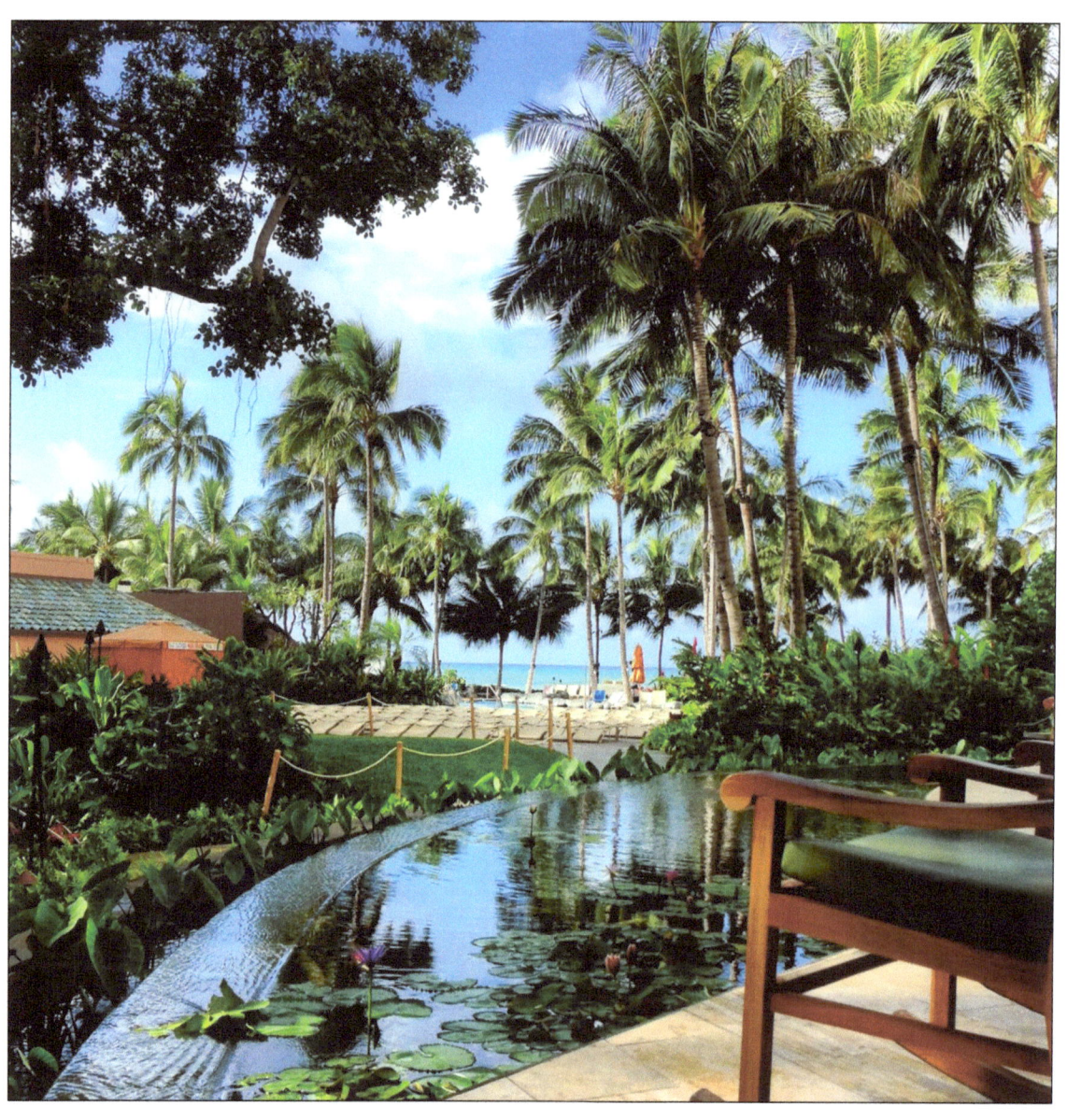

L: Paradise - Sheraton, Waikiki.
R: Paradise Lost - Hunter's Point Shipyard.

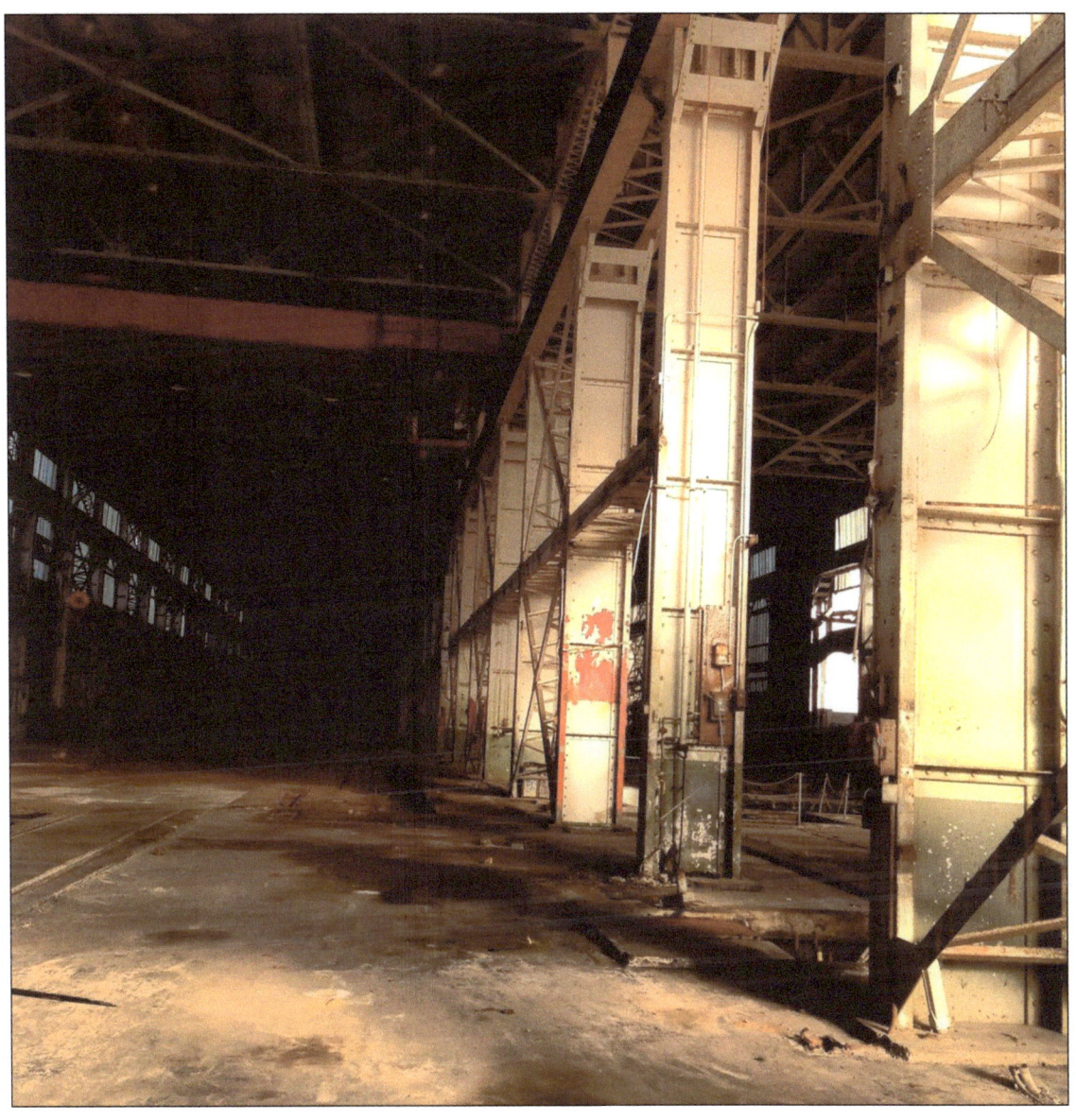

...it is true, even people with painful childhoods...grow up to be more interesting people. So, there's always a positive to a negative.

—Barbra Streisand

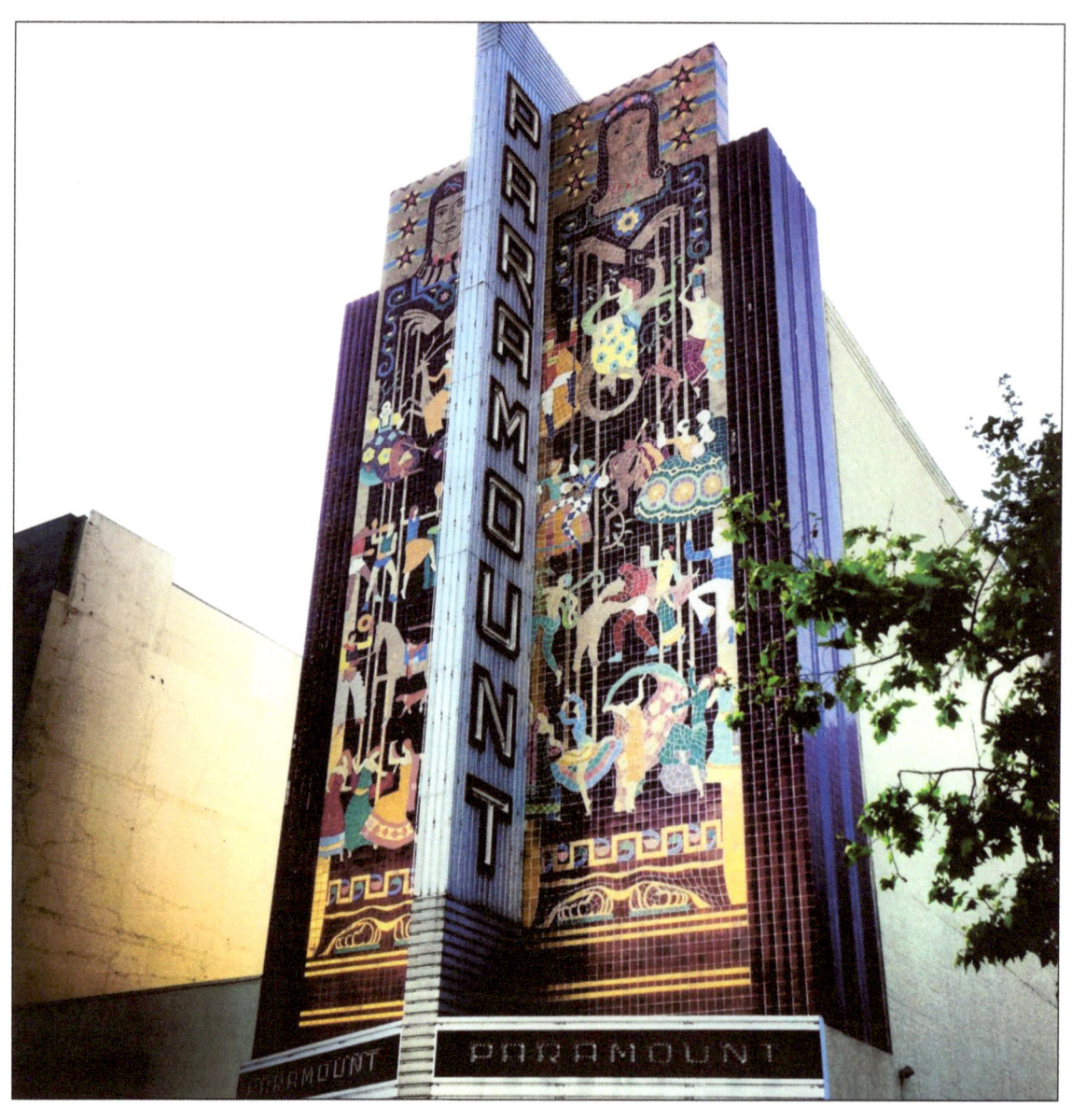

L: Paramount Theater, Down Town Oakland.
R: Oakland Tribune, Downtown Oakland.

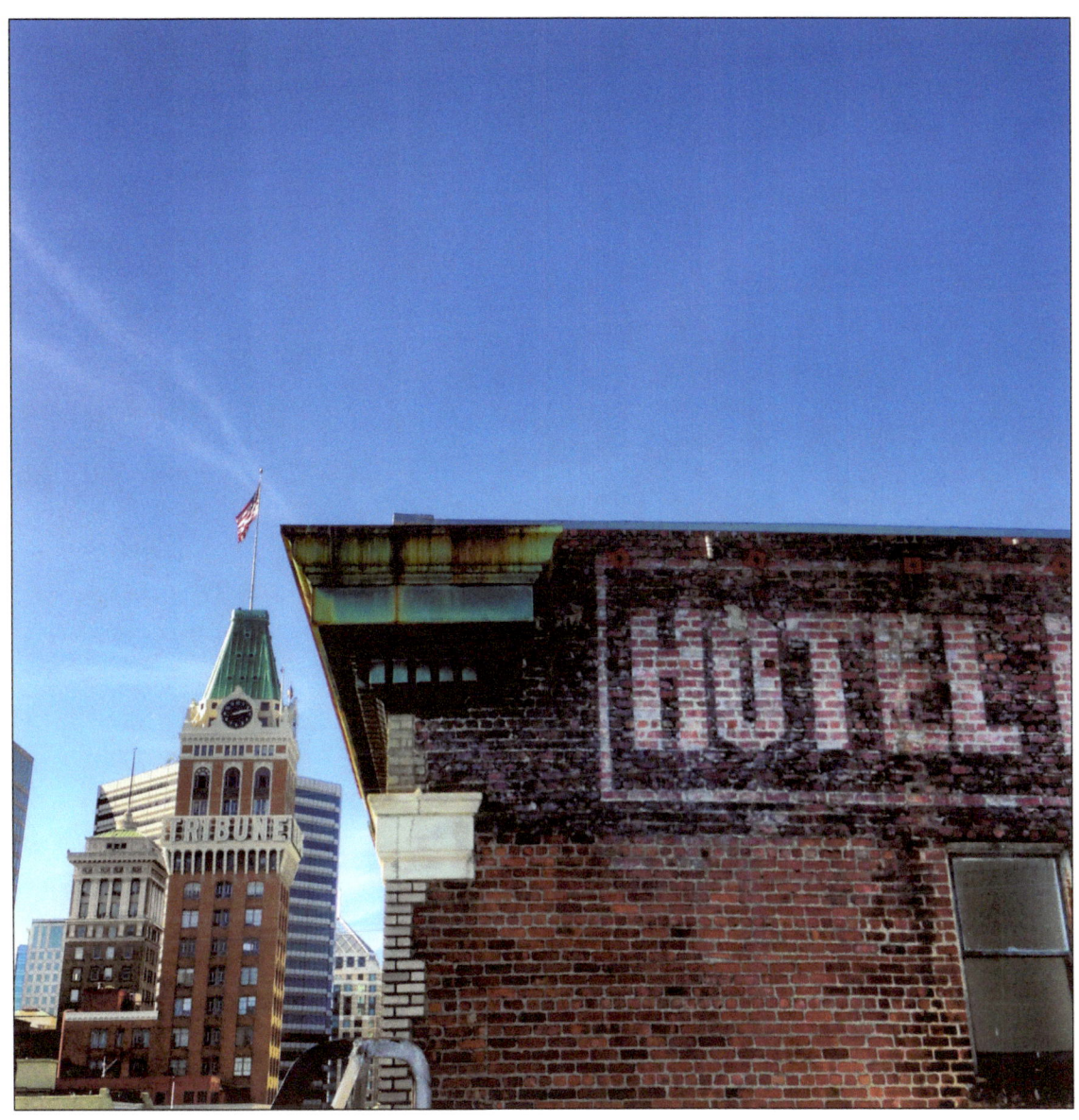

I was the shyest human ever invented, but I had a
lion inside me that wouldn't shut up.

—Ingrid Bergman

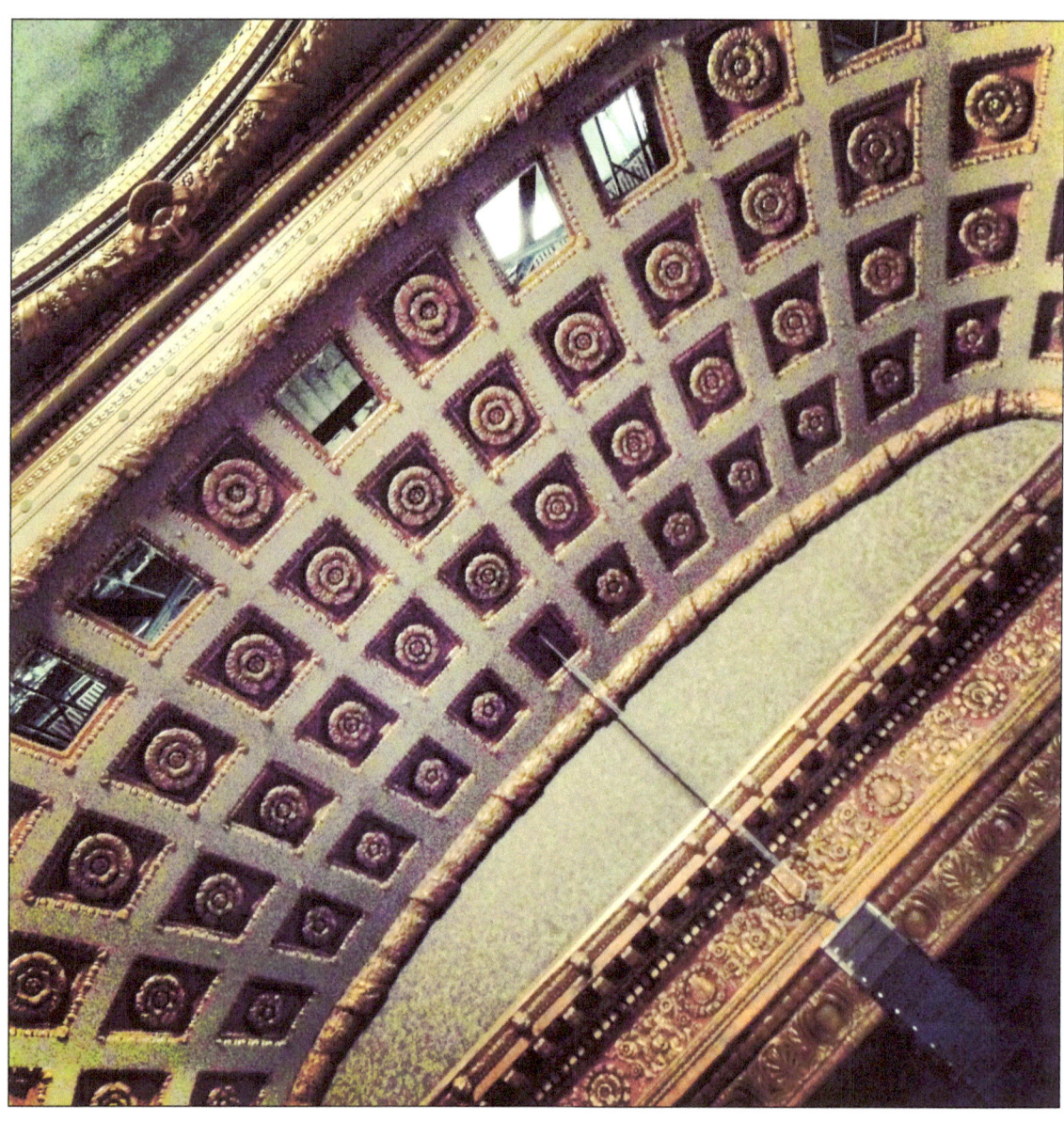

L: American Conservatory Theater, San Francisco.
R: War Memorial Opera House, San Francisco.

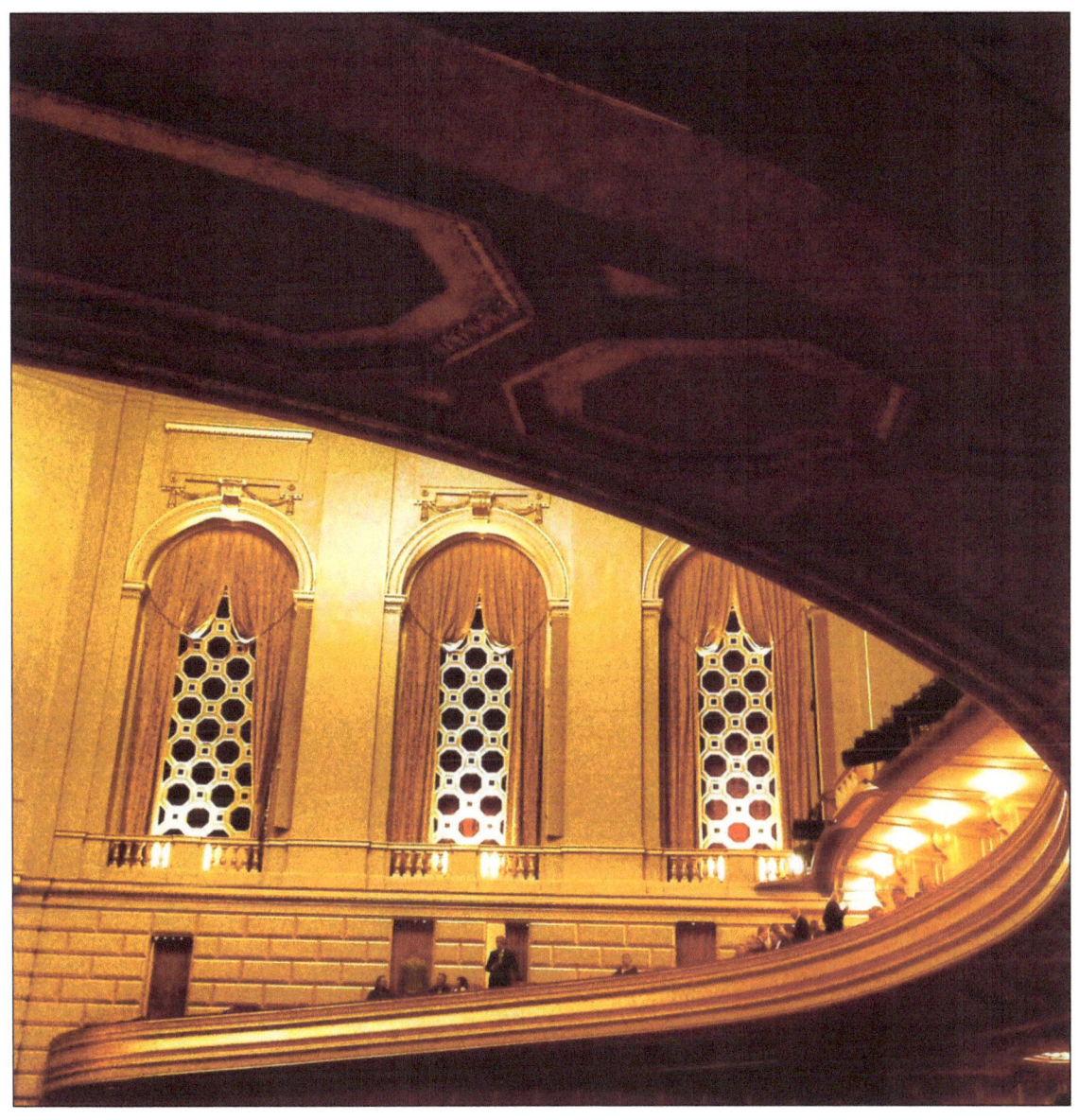

Just because you fail once doesn't mean you're gonna
fail at everything.

- Marilyn Monroe

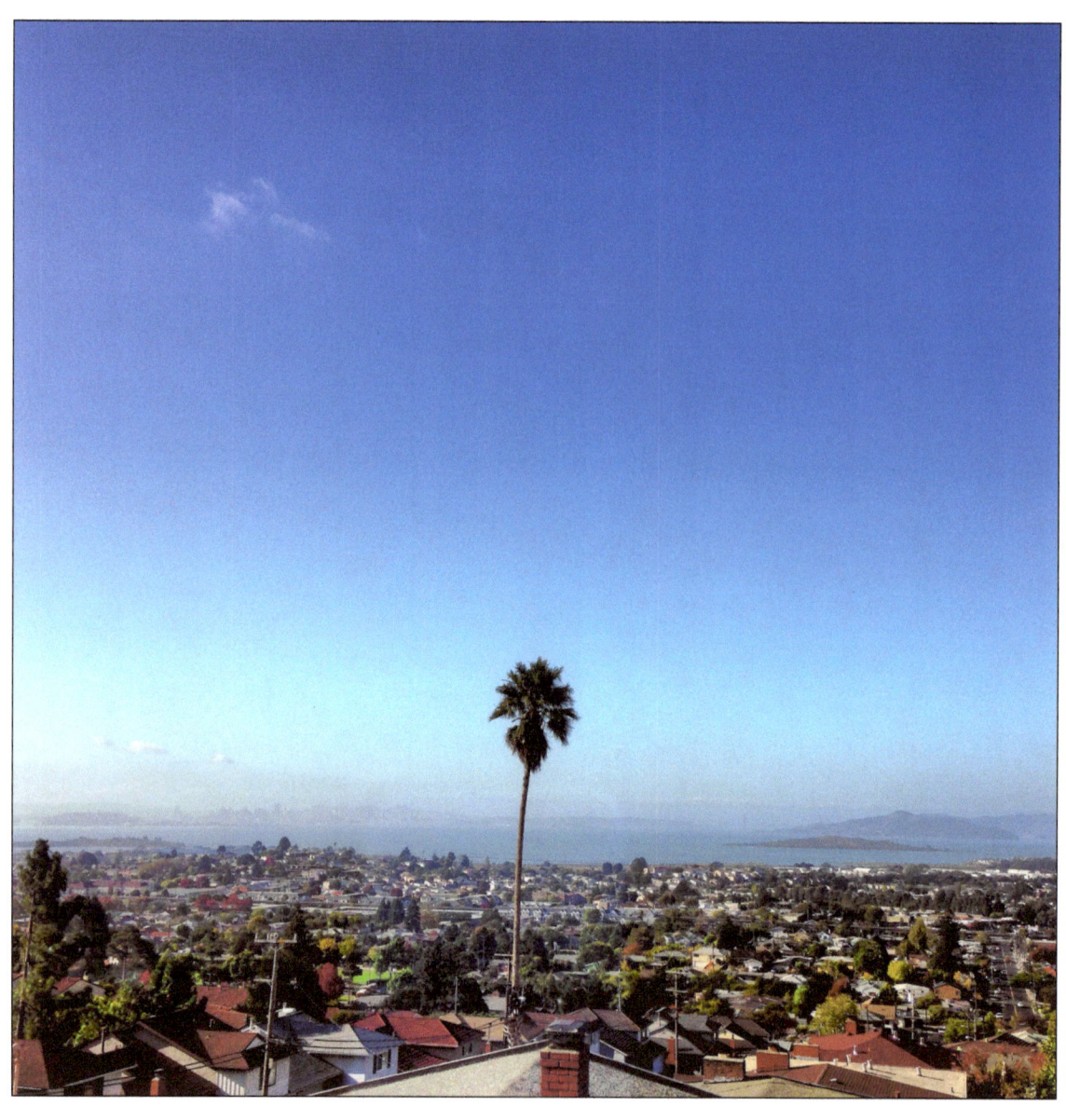

L: Palm tree against Golden Gate Bridge, East Bay.
R: Directly under the Golden Gate Bridge, San Francisco.

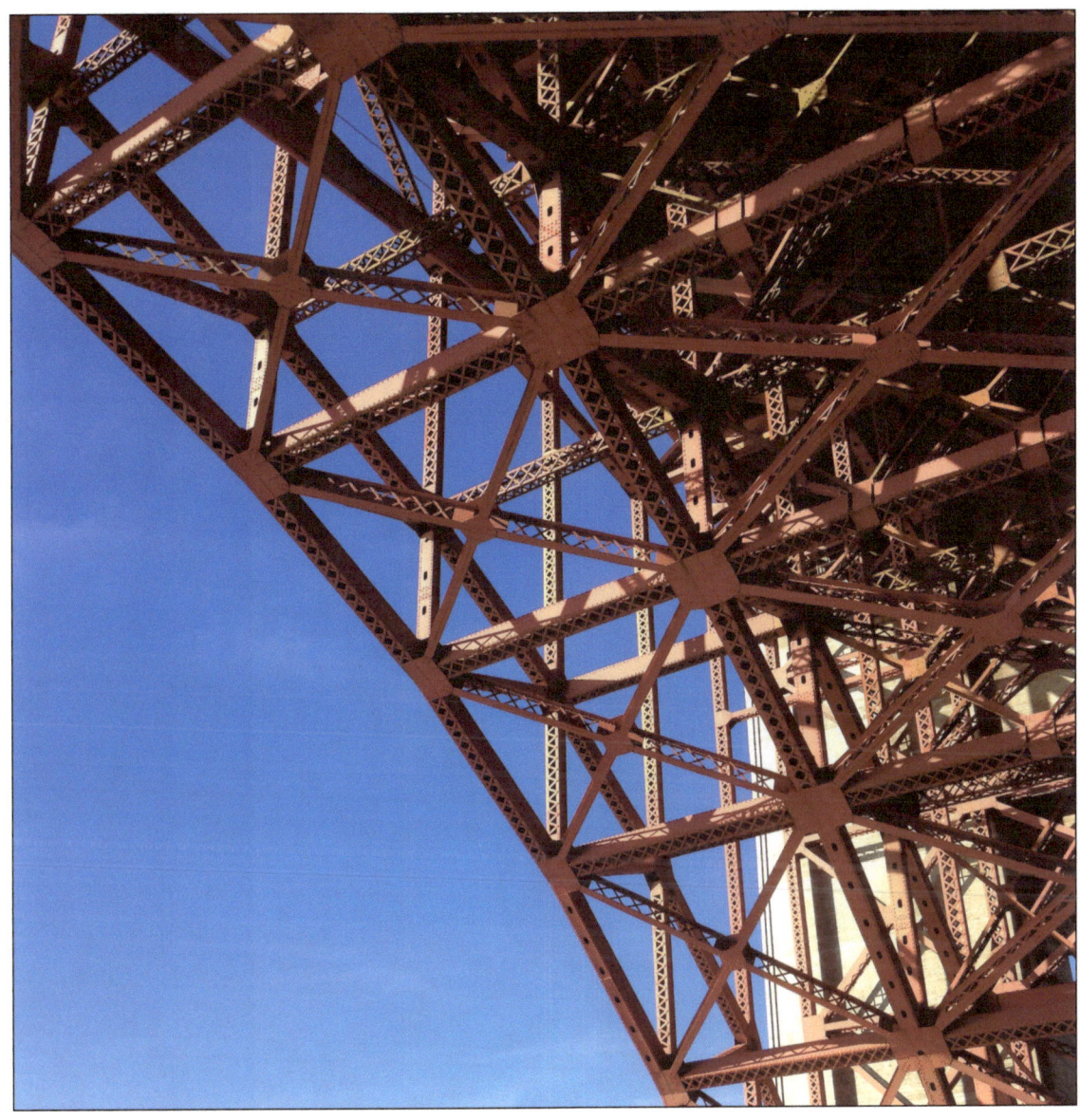

You should know me well enough by now to know I don't ask for things I don't think I can get.

—Marilyn Monroe

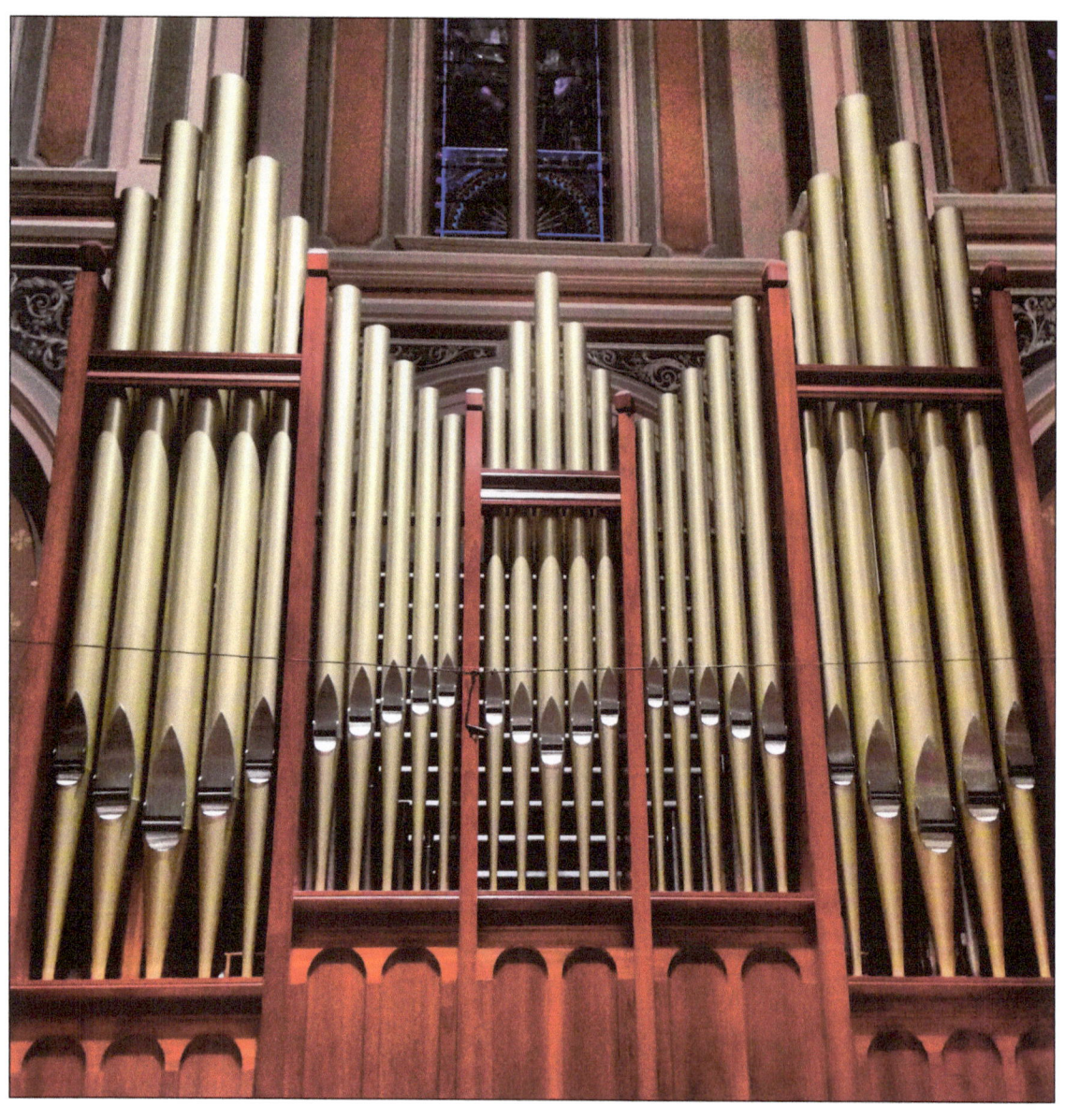

L: Cathedral of the Blessed sacrament, Sacramento.
R: Asian Art Museum, San Francisco.

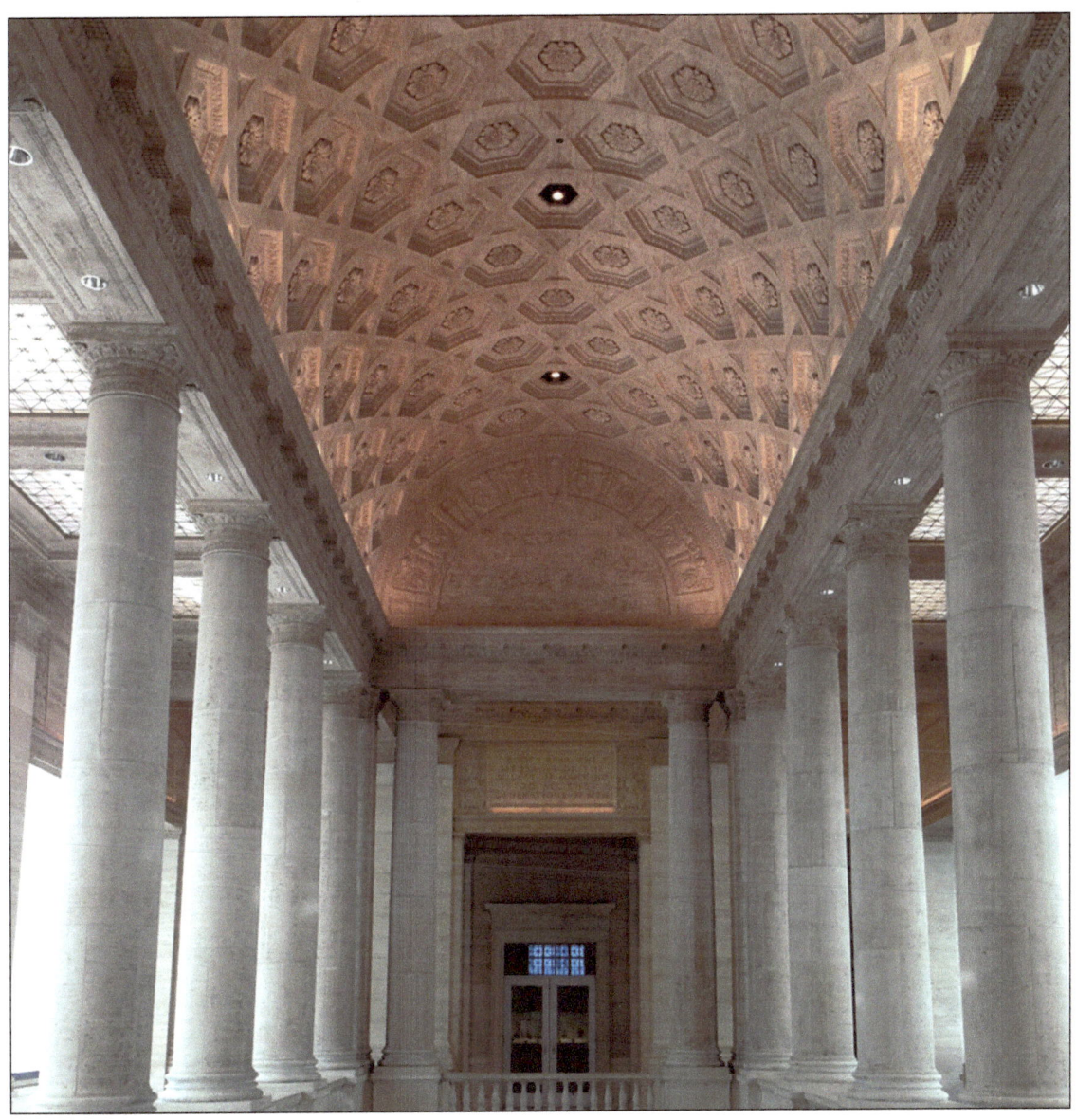

I have learned to love that which is meant to harm me, so that I can stand in the way of those who are less strong. I can take the bullets for those who aren't able to.

—Margaret Cho

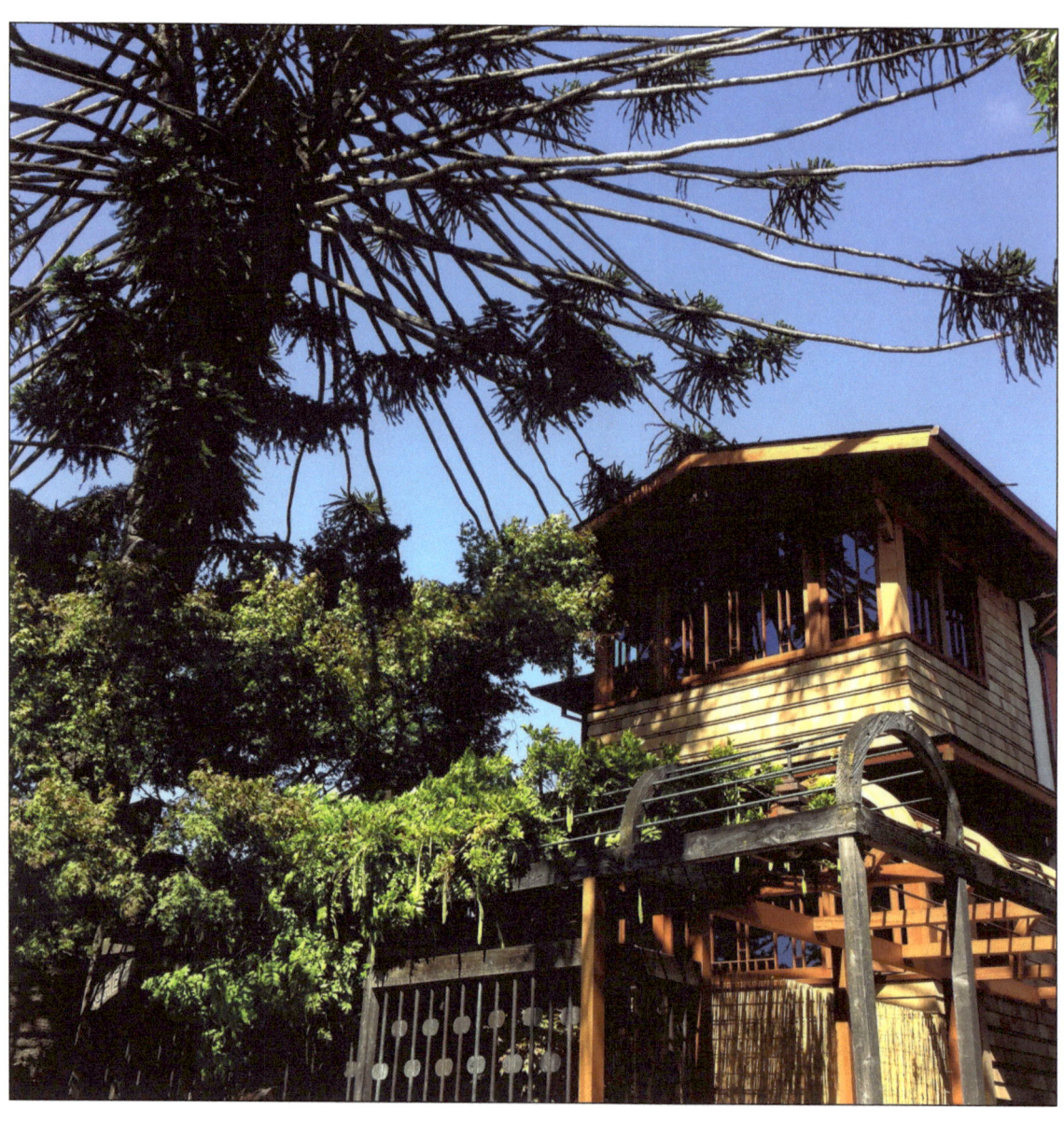

L: Chez Panisse, Gourmet Ghetto, Berkeley.
R: Waikiki, Honolulu.

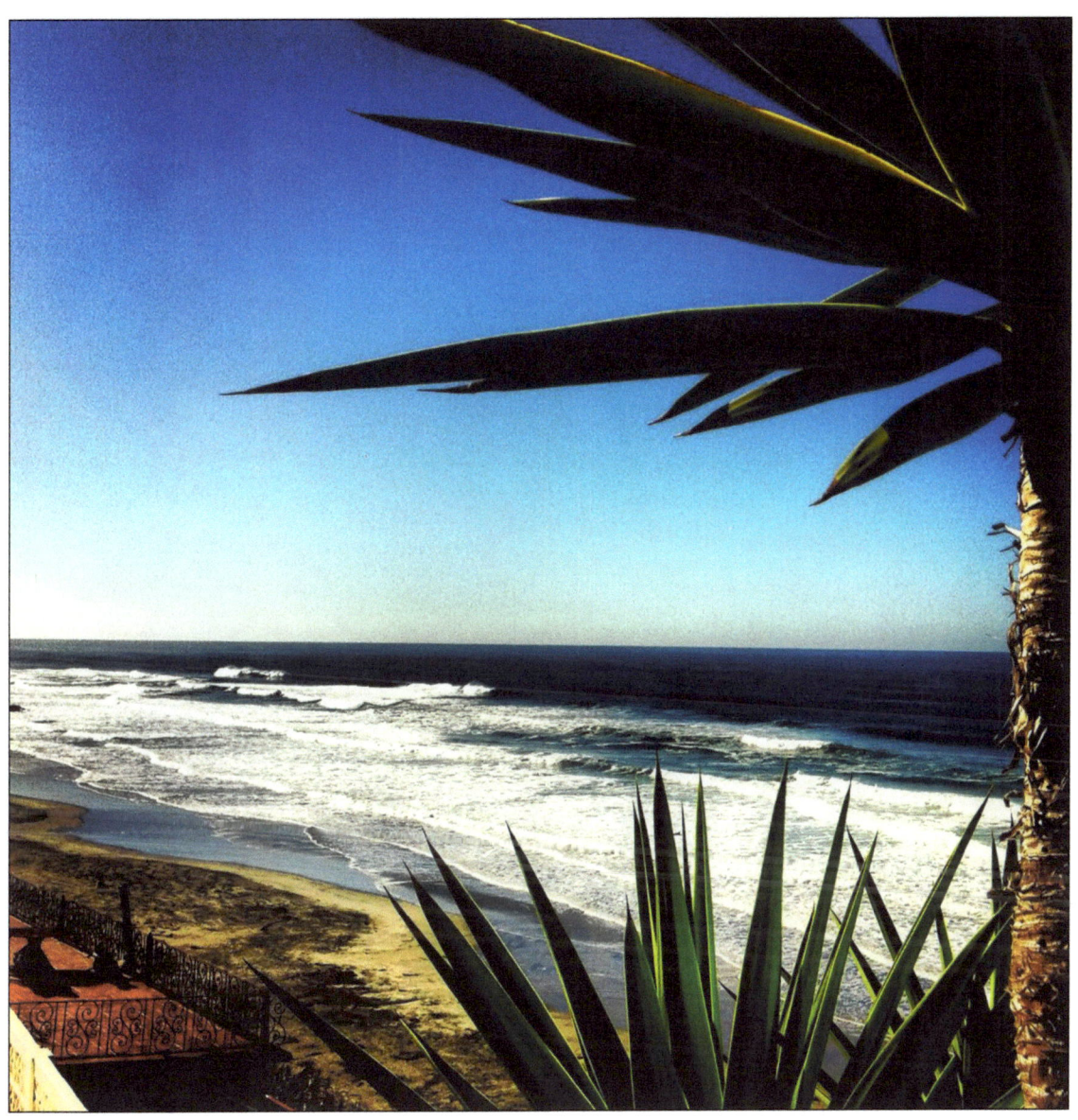

I'm not intimidated by anyone. Everyone is made with two arms, two legs, a stomach and a head. Just think about that.

—Josephine Baker

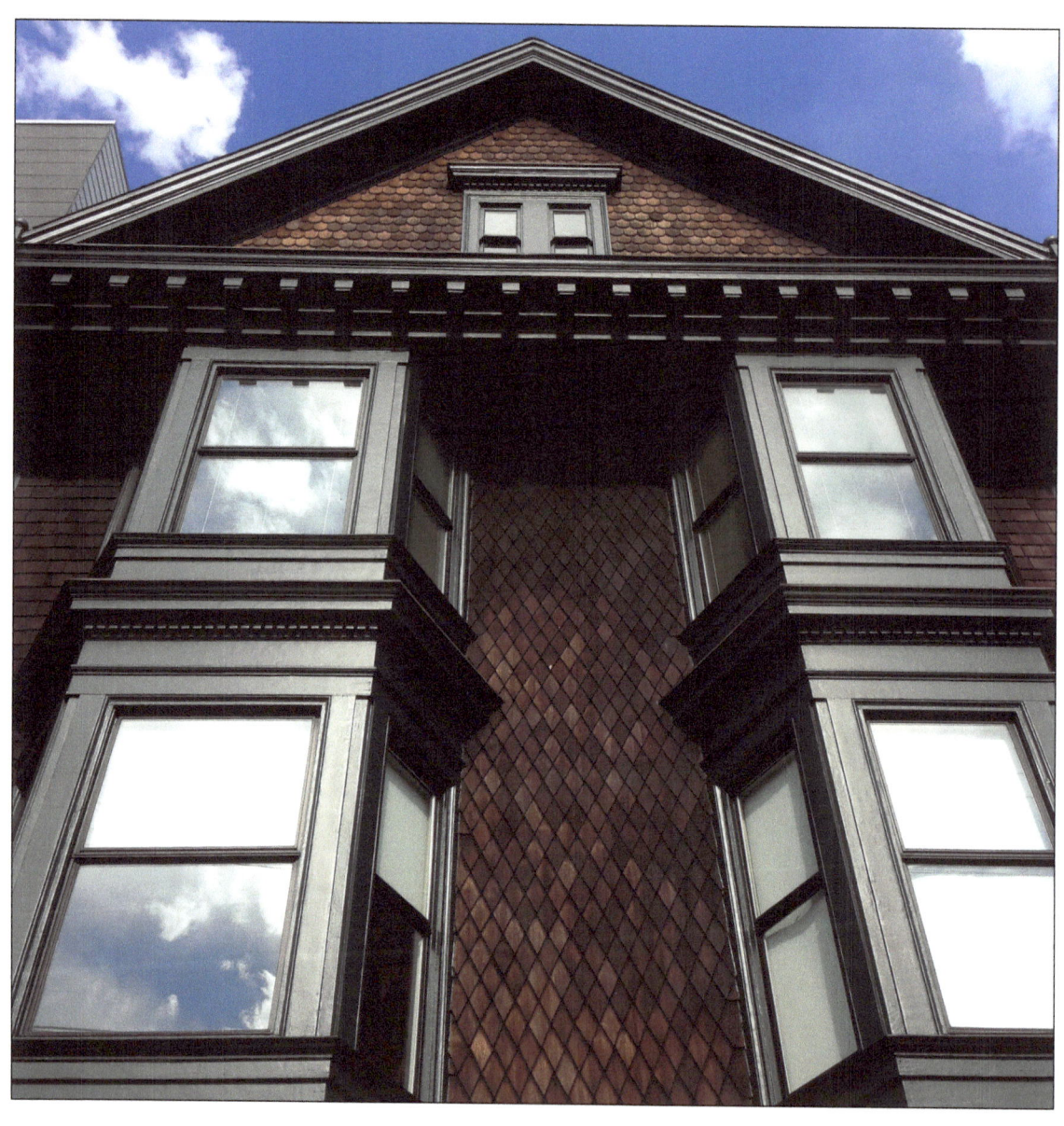

L: Castro, San Francisco.
R: Jack London Square, Oakland.

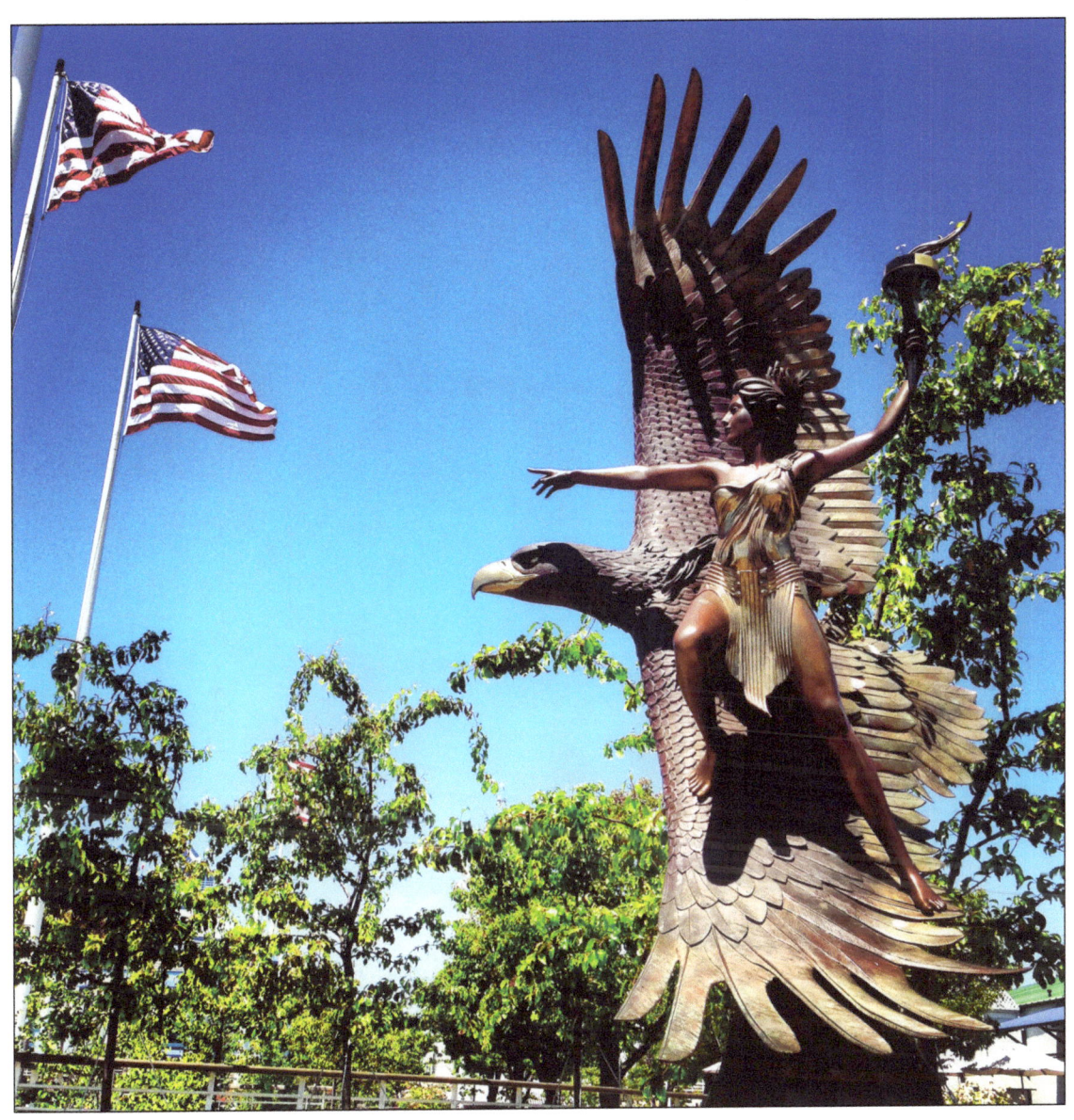

A dame that knows the ropes isn't likely to get tied up.

—Mae West

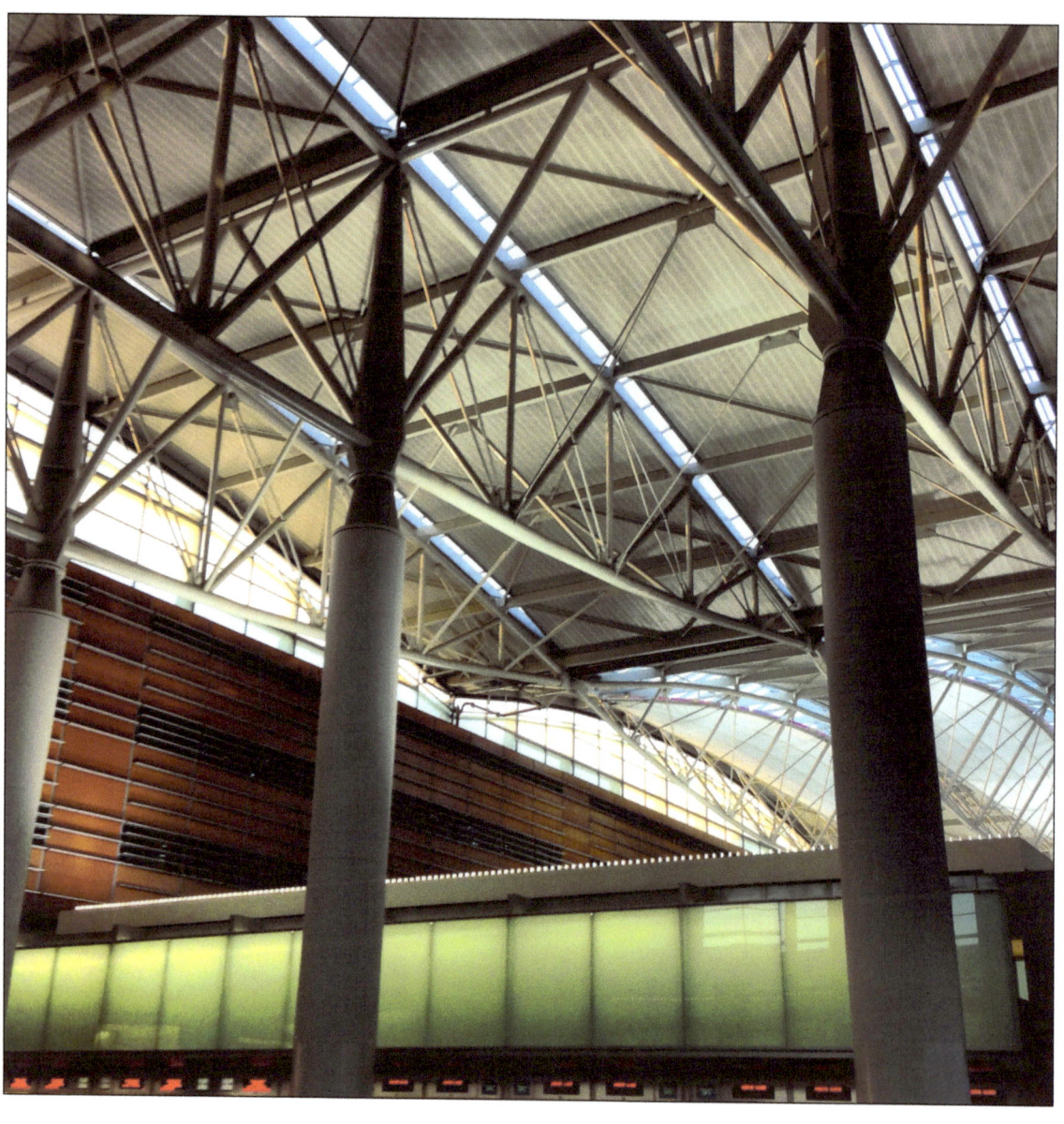

L: Concrete Branches, SFO
R: Wood Branches, North Berkeley.

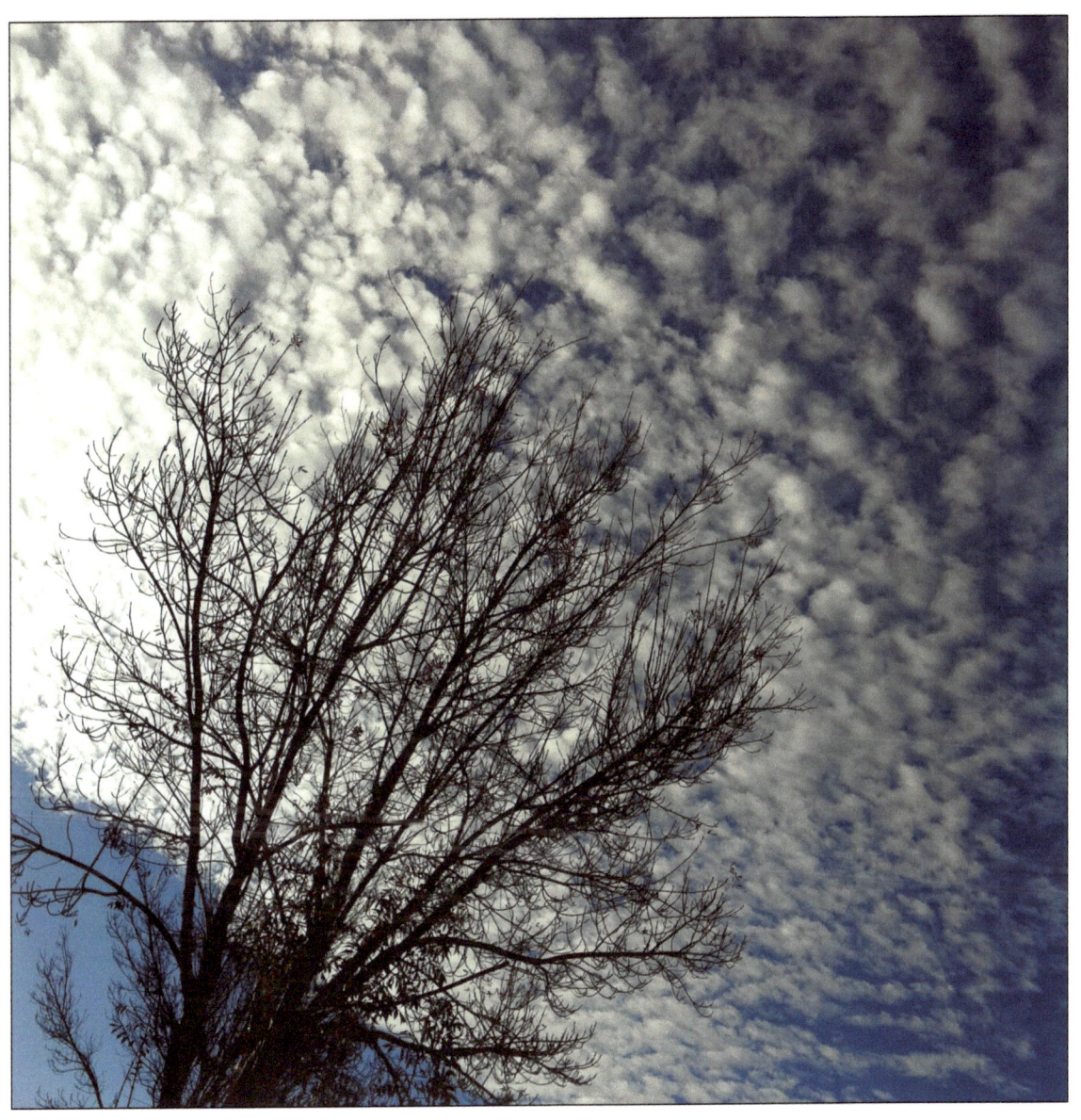

A sure way to lose happiness, I found, is to
want it at the expense of everything else.

—Bette Davis

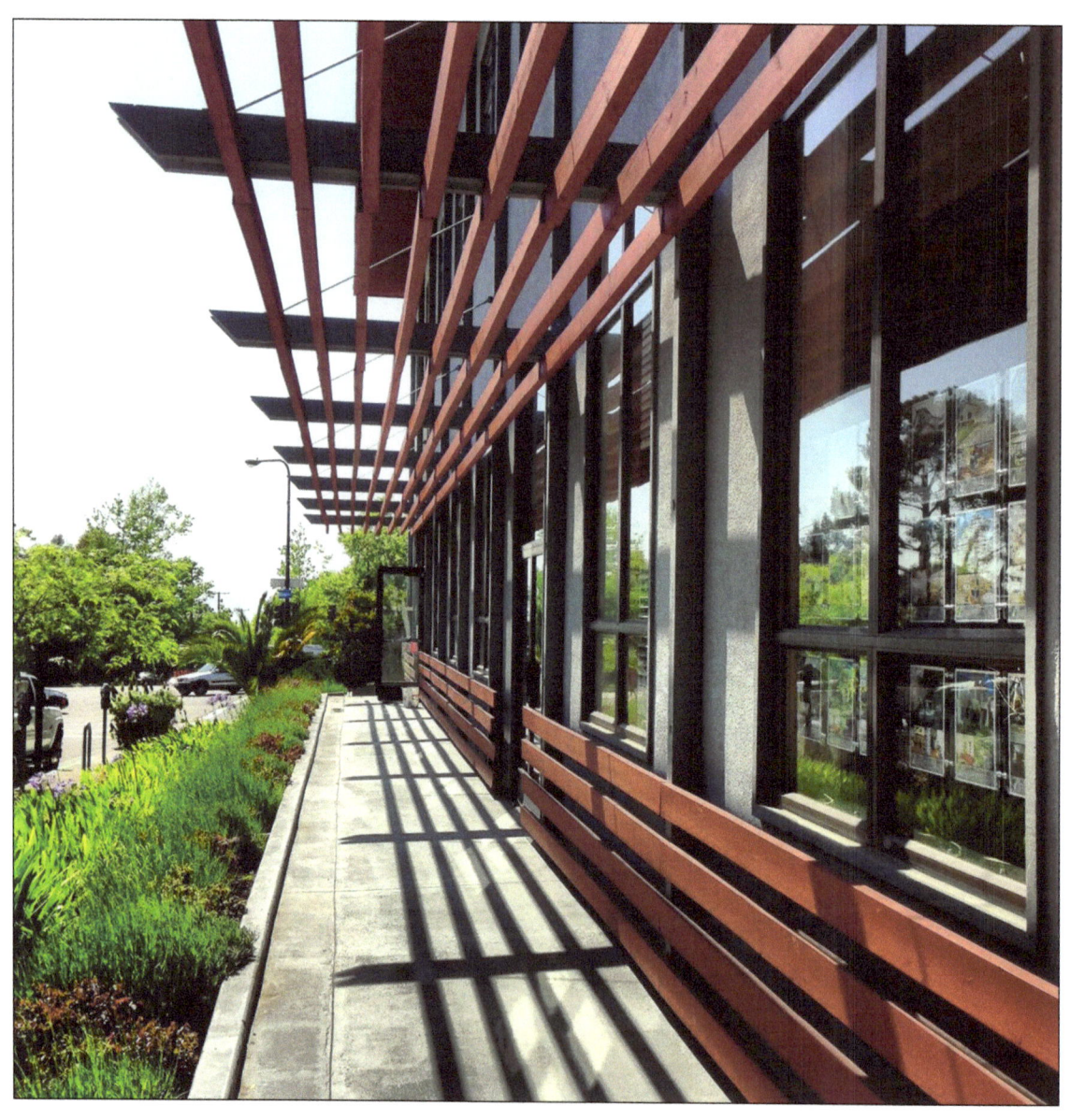

L: Better Homer & Gardens Real Estate, Berkeley, California.
R: 4th Street Caltrain Station, South of Market, San Francisco.

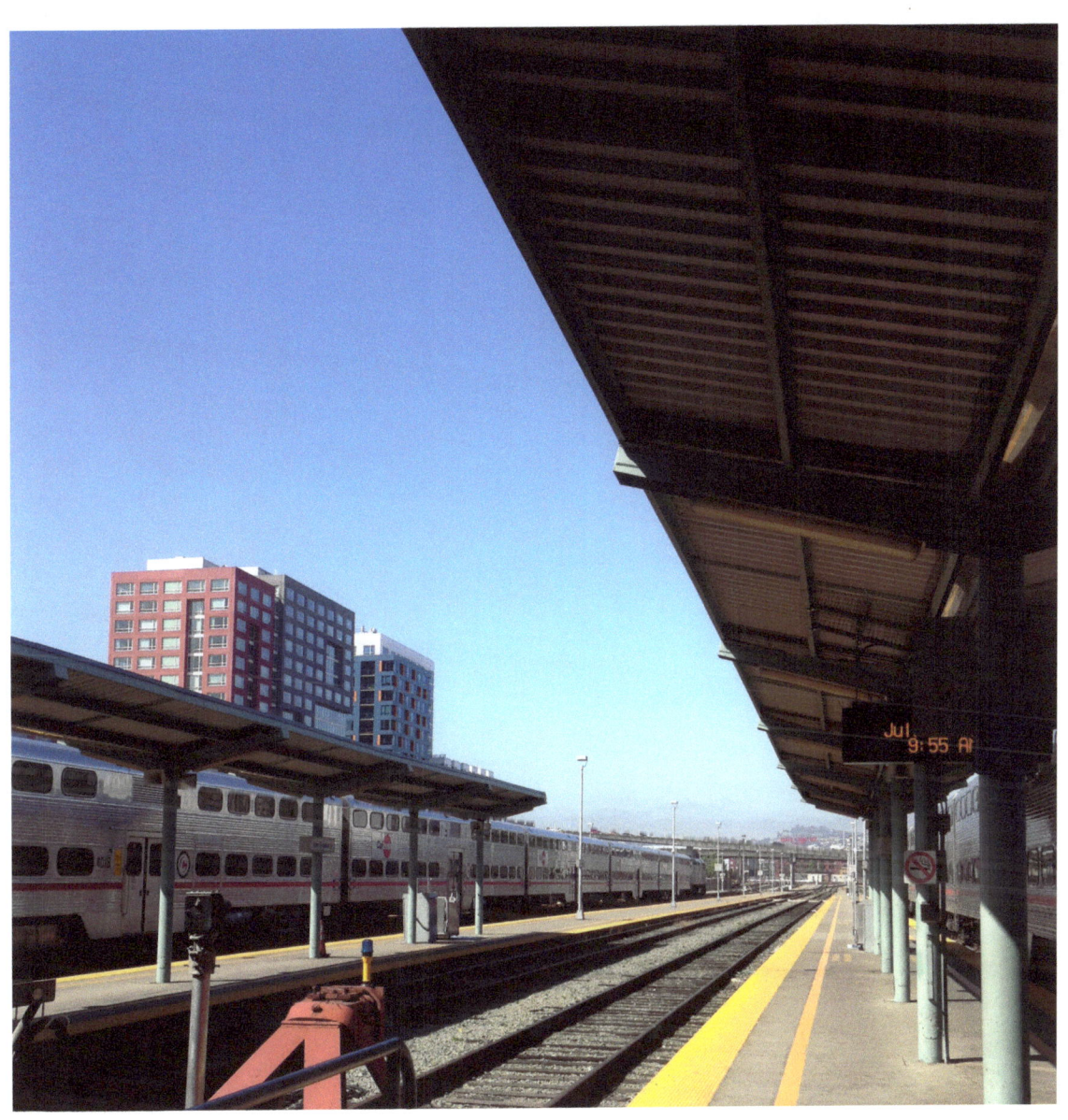

Fashion is architecture: it is a matter of proportions.

—Coco Chanel

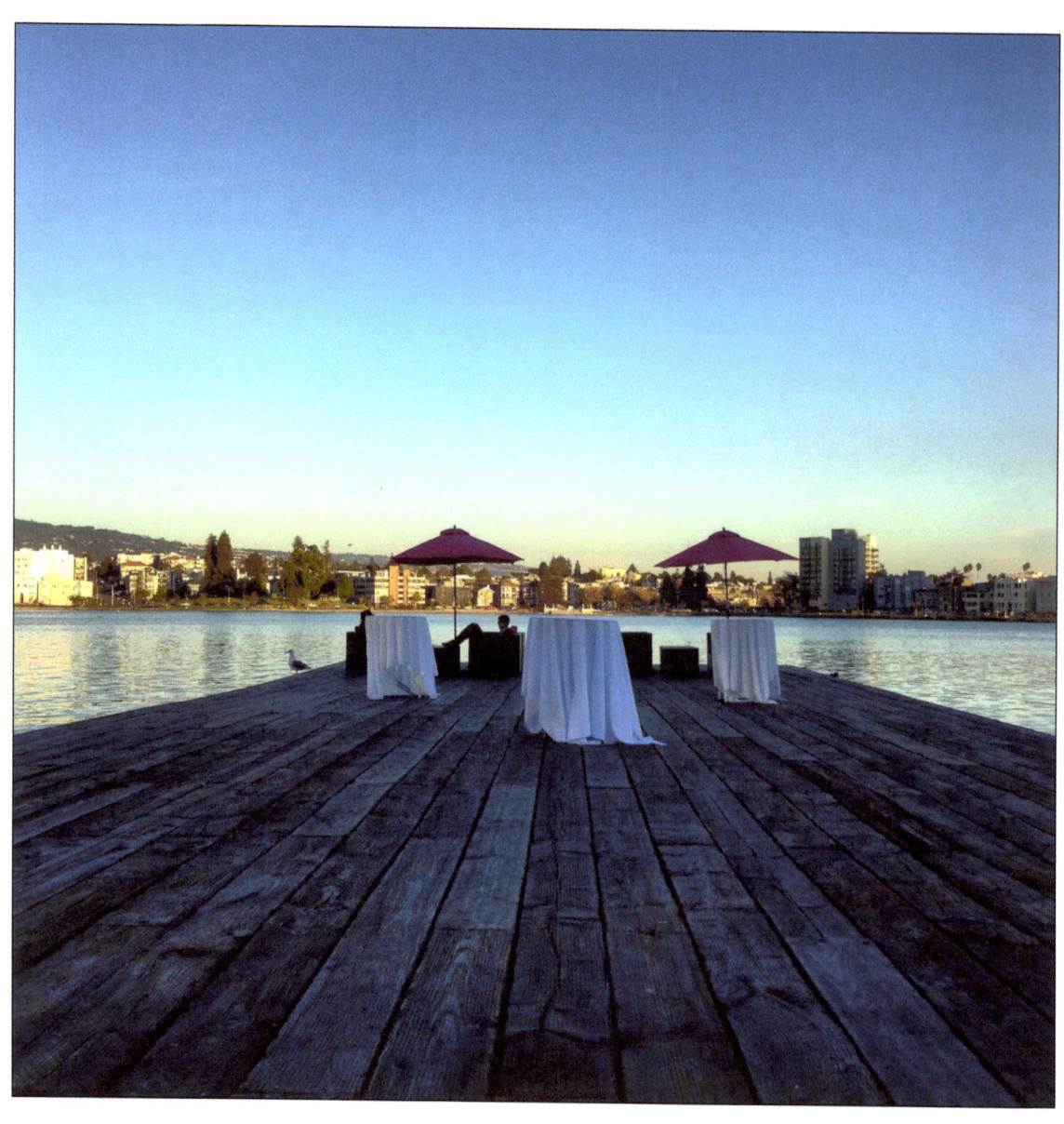

L: The Lake Chalet Seafood Bar & Grill, Lake Merritt, Oarkland.
R: San Francisco Federal Building.

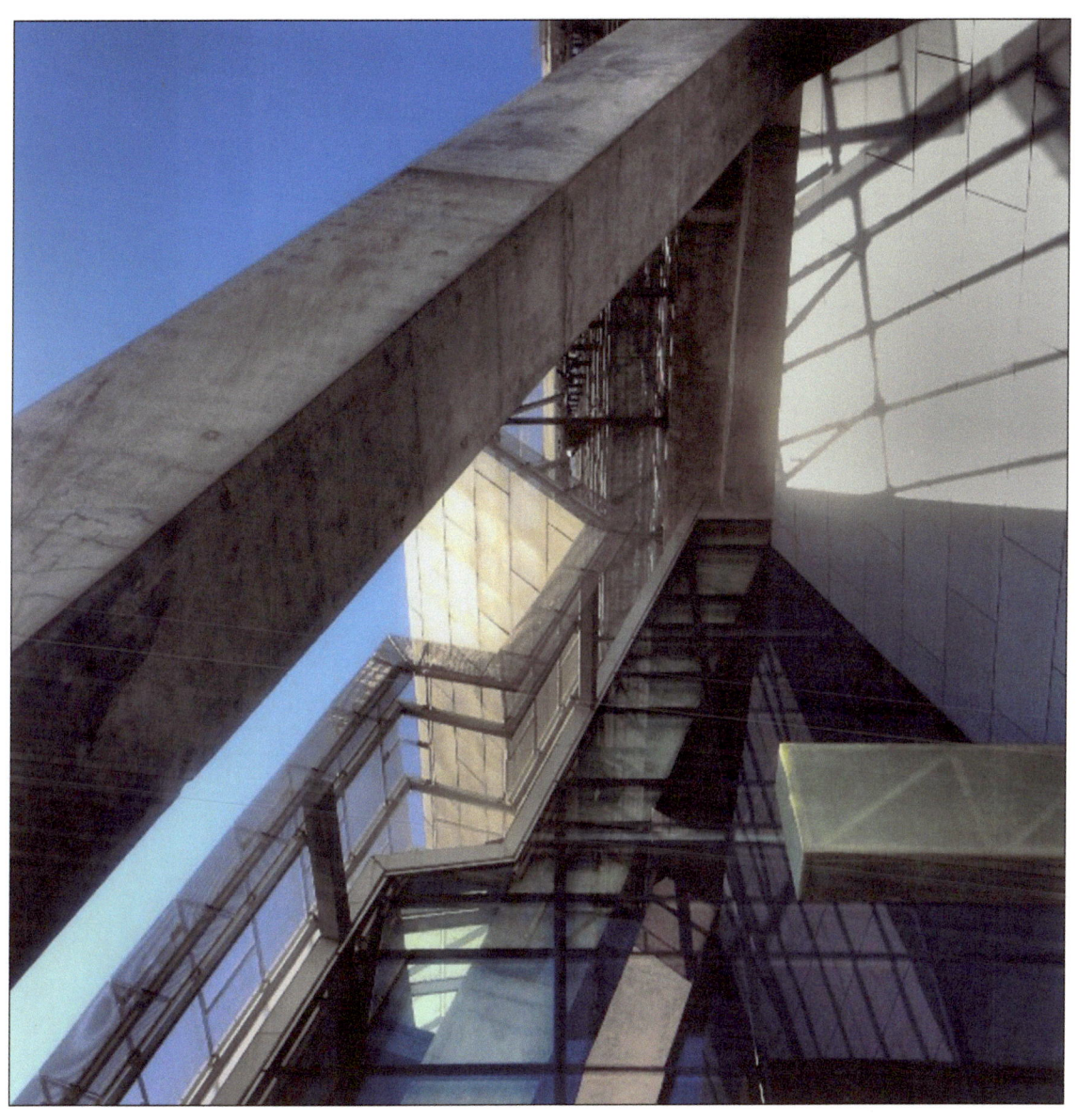

It's the friends you can call up at 4 am that matter.

—Marlene Dietrich

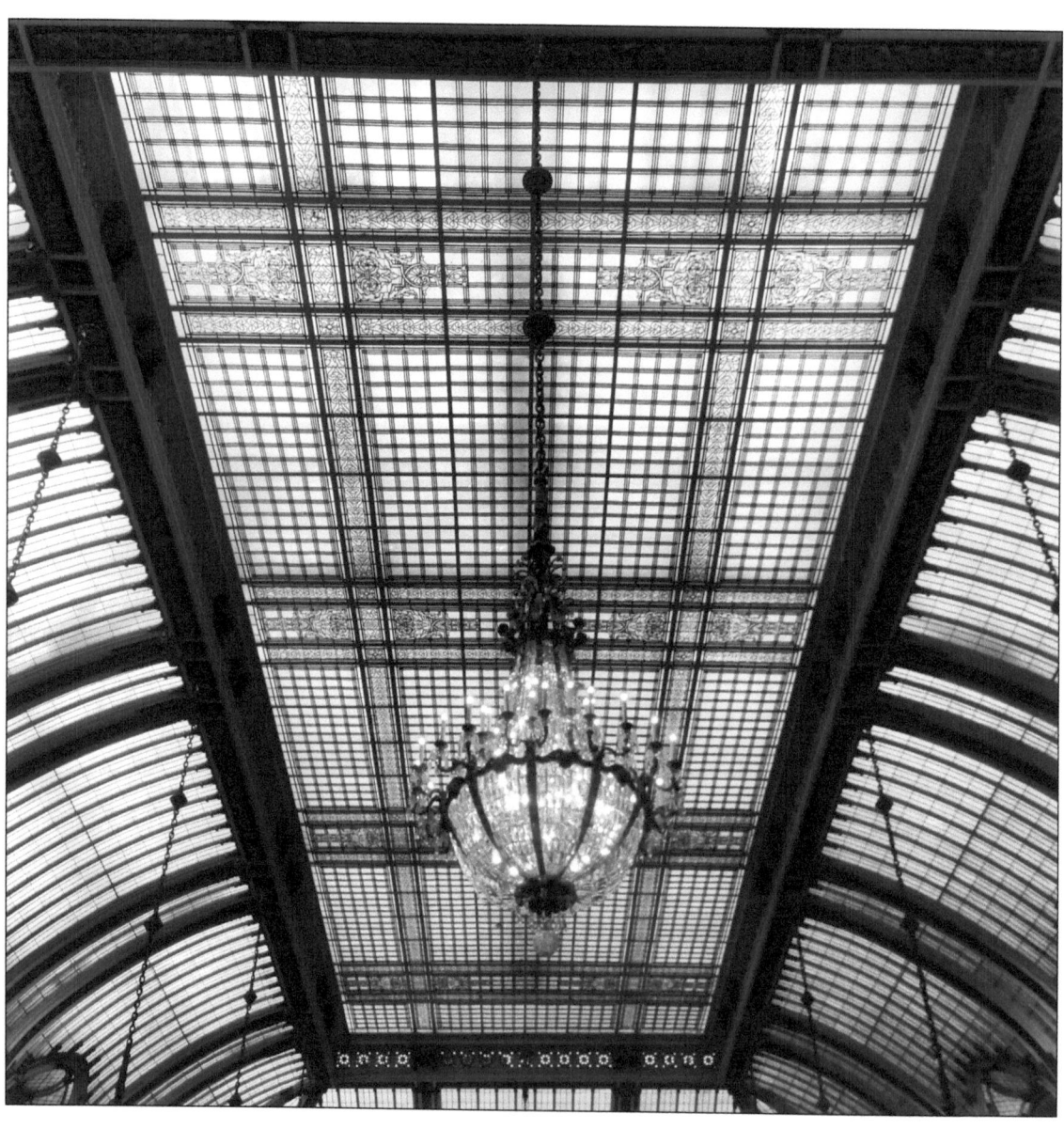

L & R: A Tale of Two Ceilings, The Palace Hotel, San Francisco.

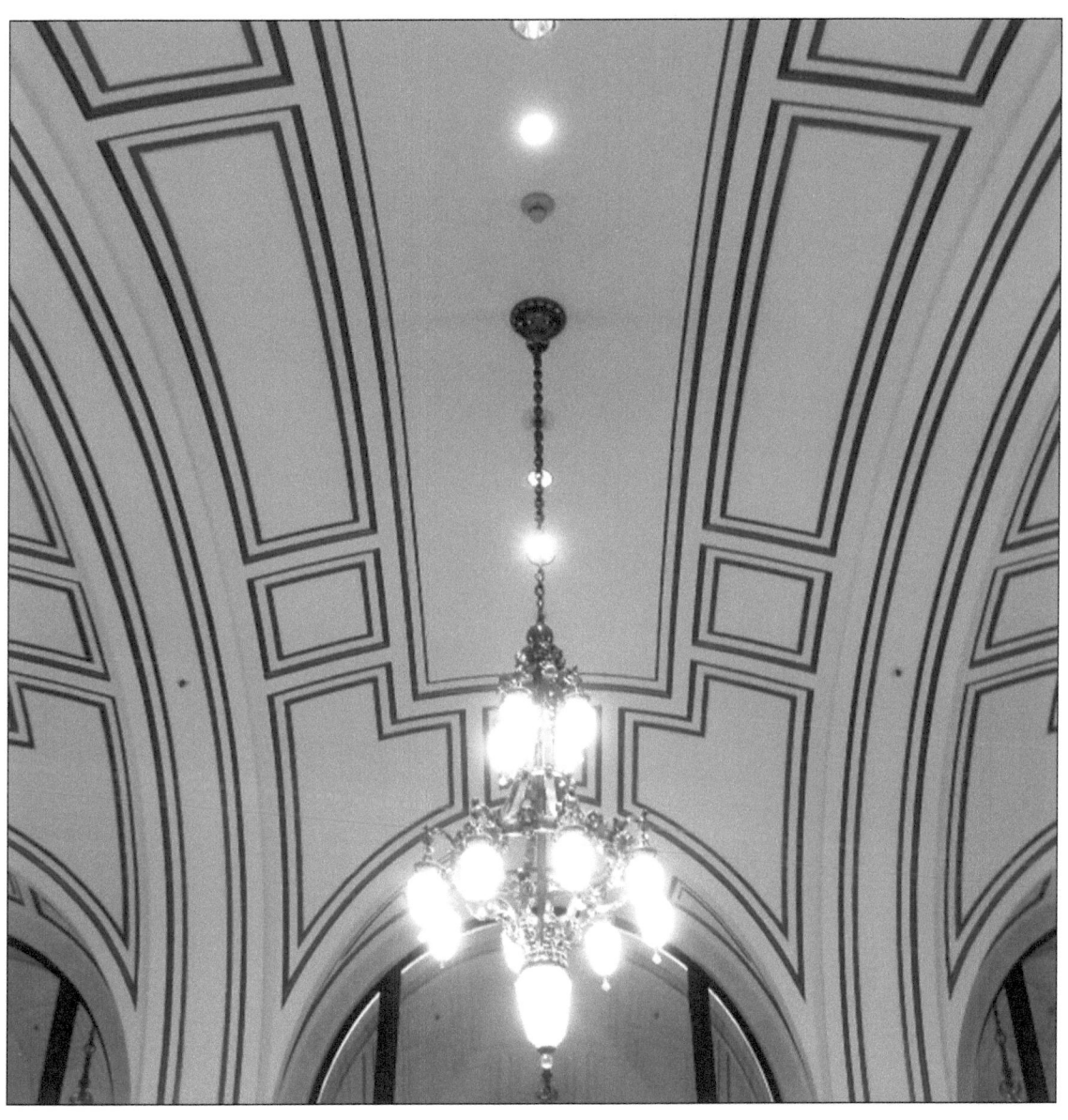

When you happy you can forgive a great deal.

—Princess Diana

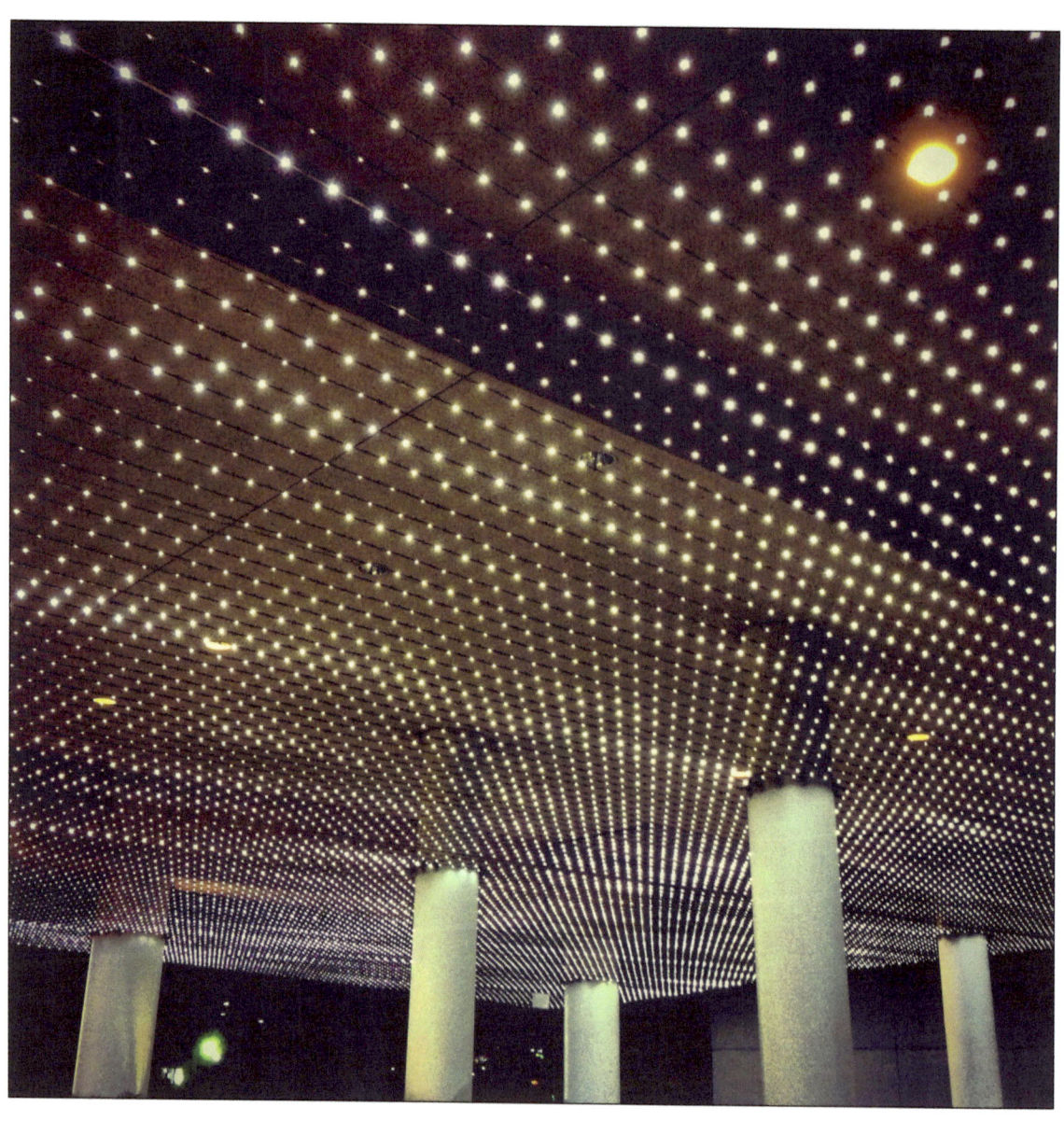

L: W Hotel, Hollywood.
R: Pandora Media Headquarters, Oakland.

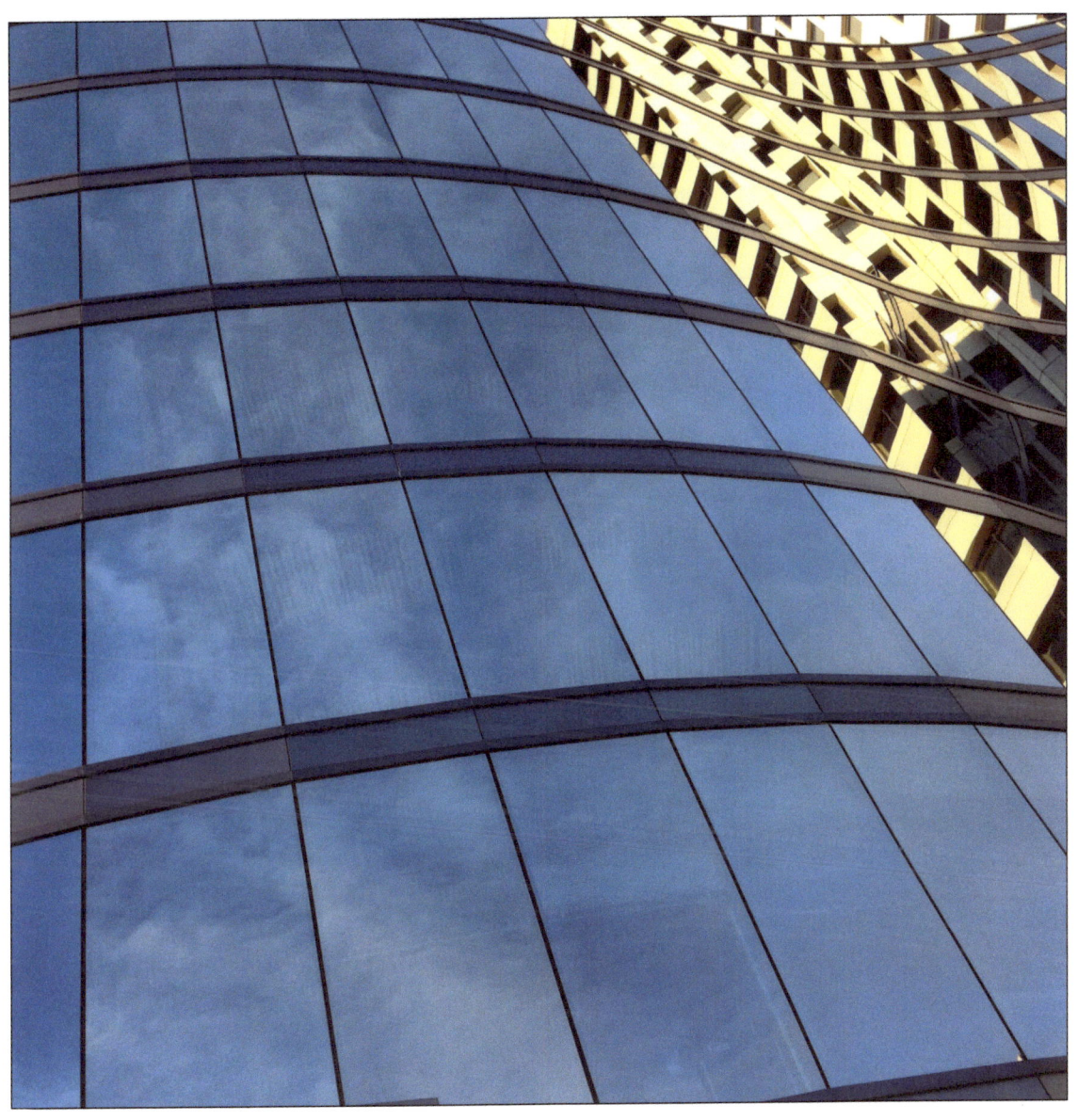

Dreaming, after all, is a form of planning.

—Gloria Steinem

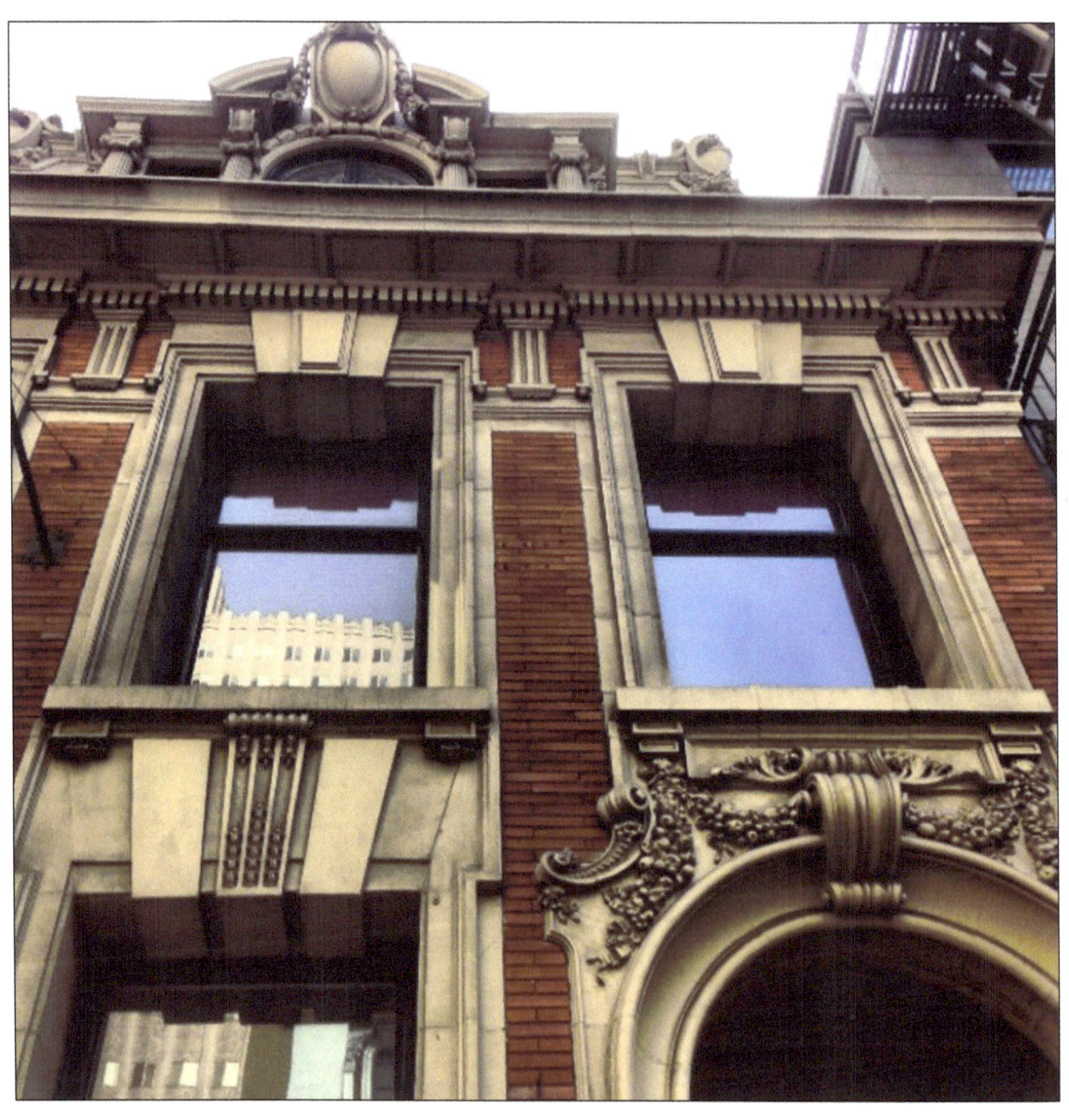

L: Hobb Hill, San Francisco.
R: Independent bookstore, Piedmont Avenue, Oakland.

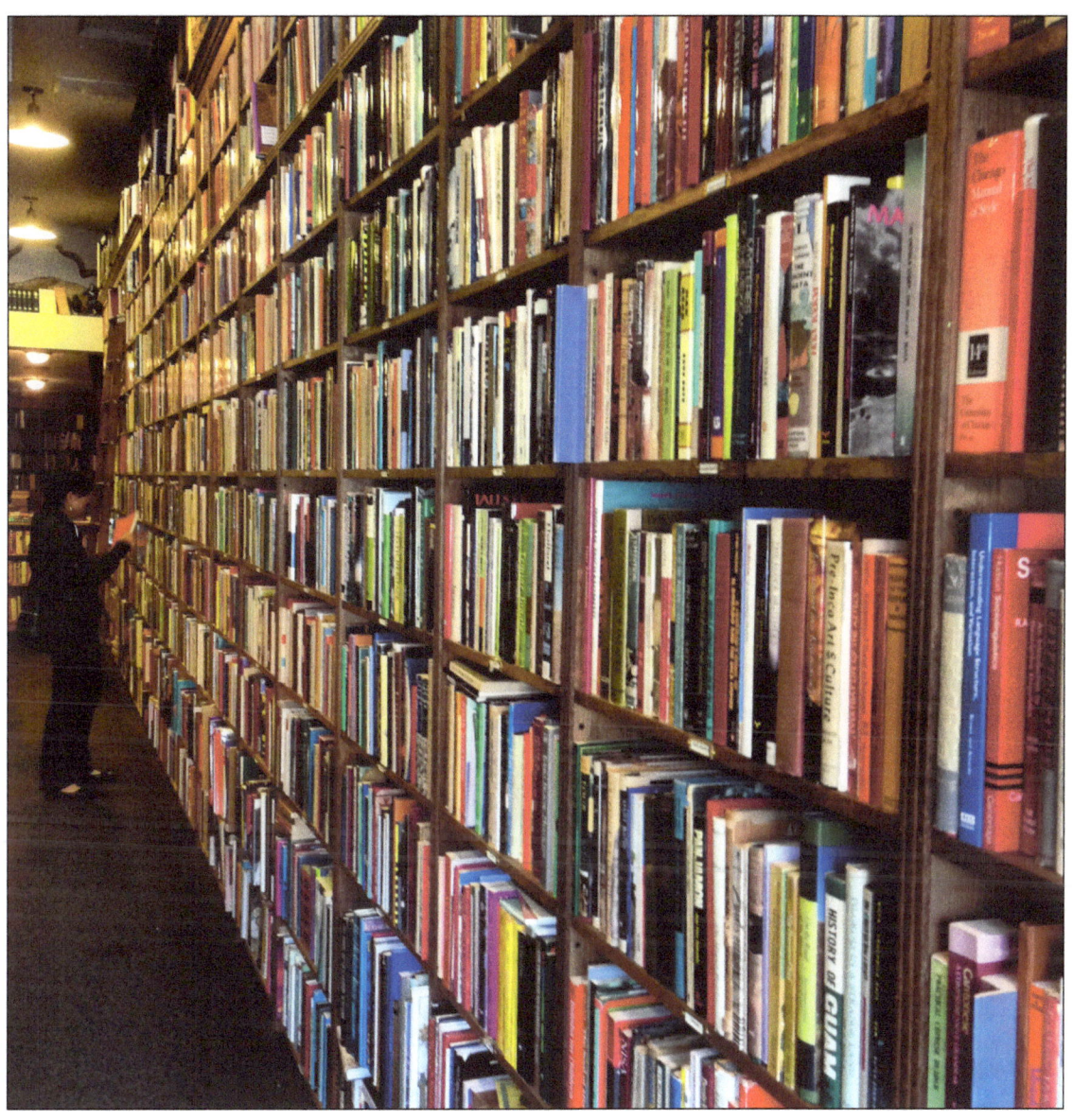

Books are like mirrors: if a fool looks in, you cannot
expect a genius to look out.

—J.K. Rowling

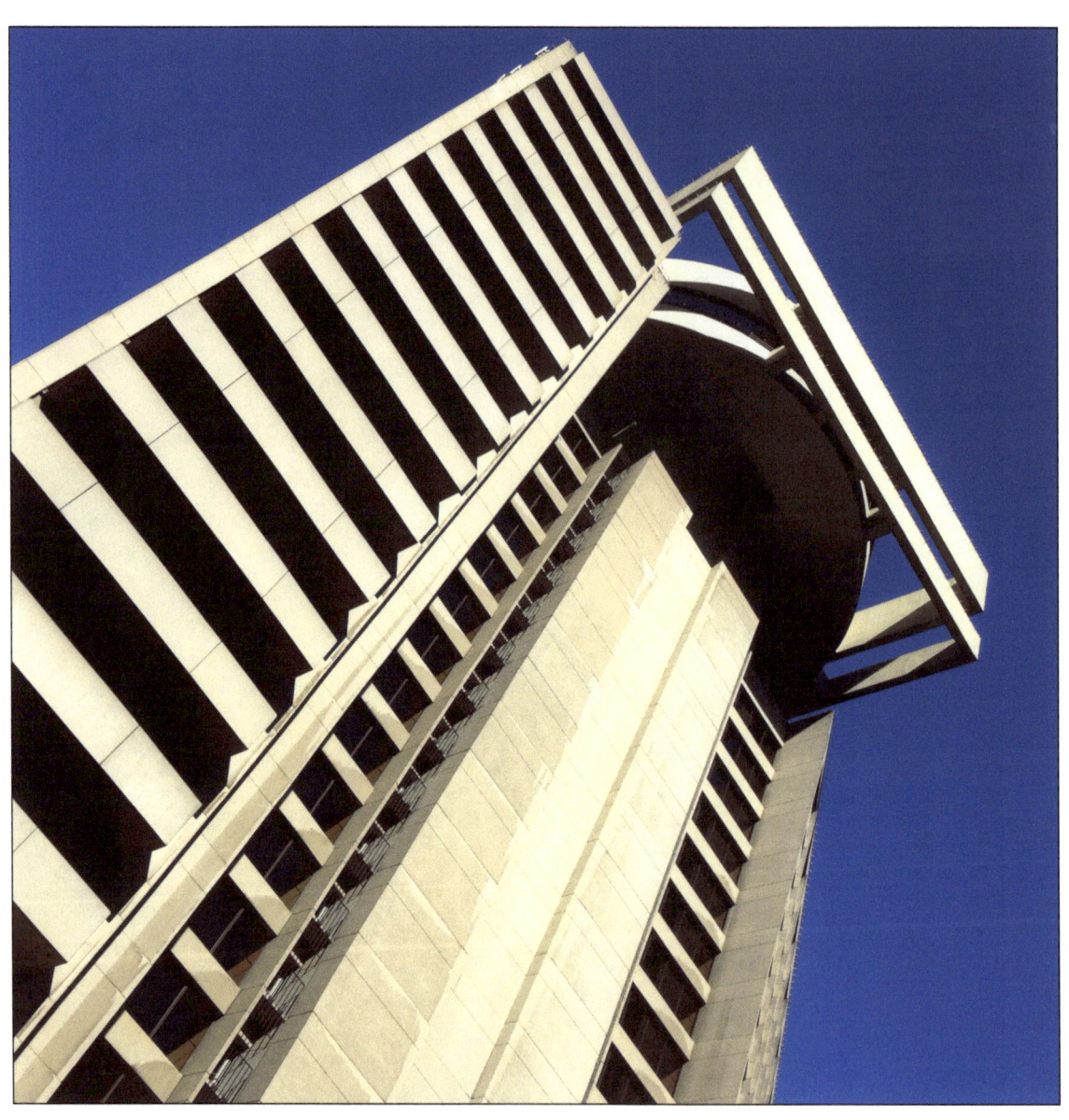

L: Hyatt Regency San Francisco.
R: Philz Coffee, Berkeley.

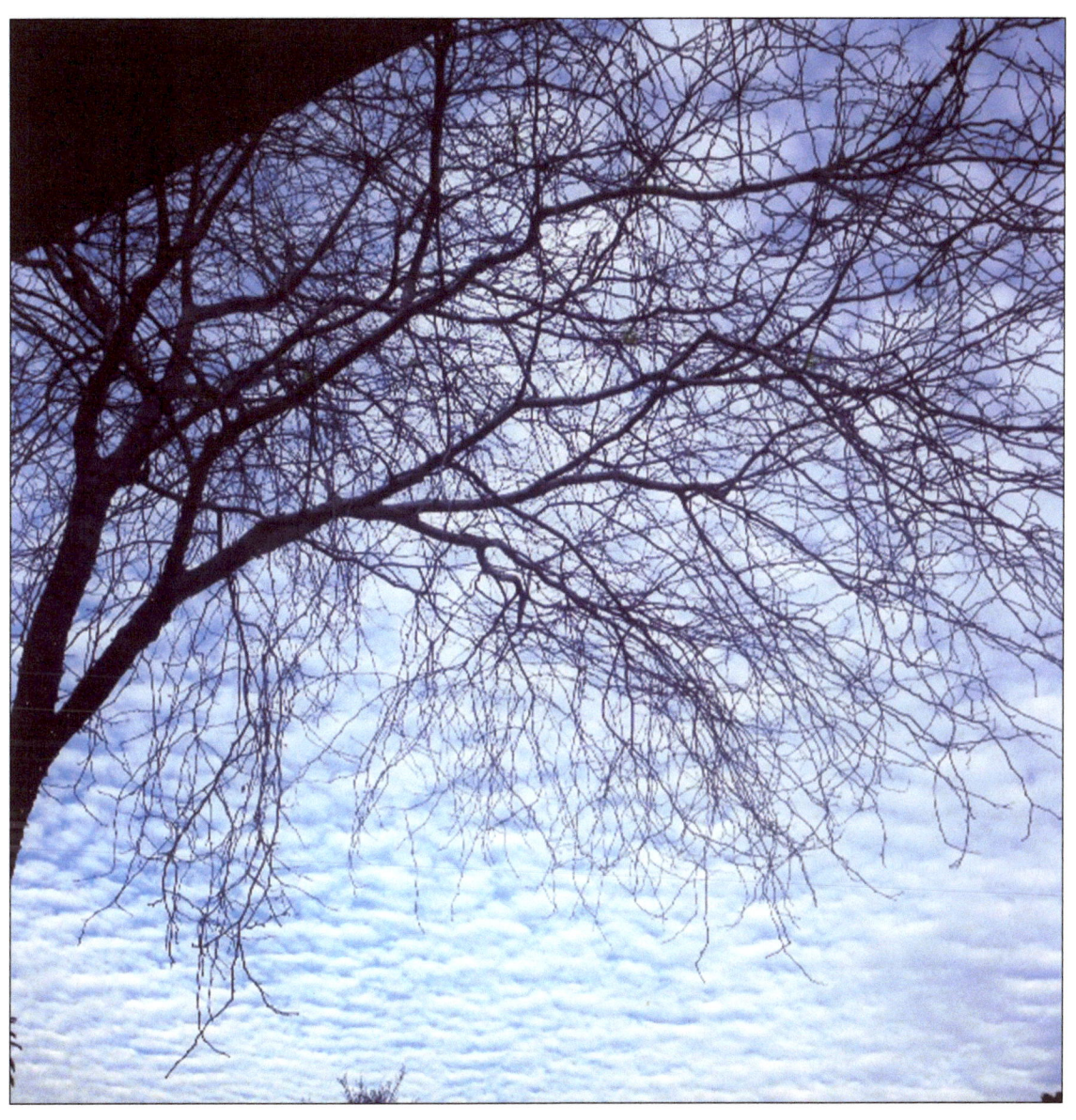

When people say: She's got everything. I've only one
answer: I haven't had tomorrow.

—Elizabeth Taylor

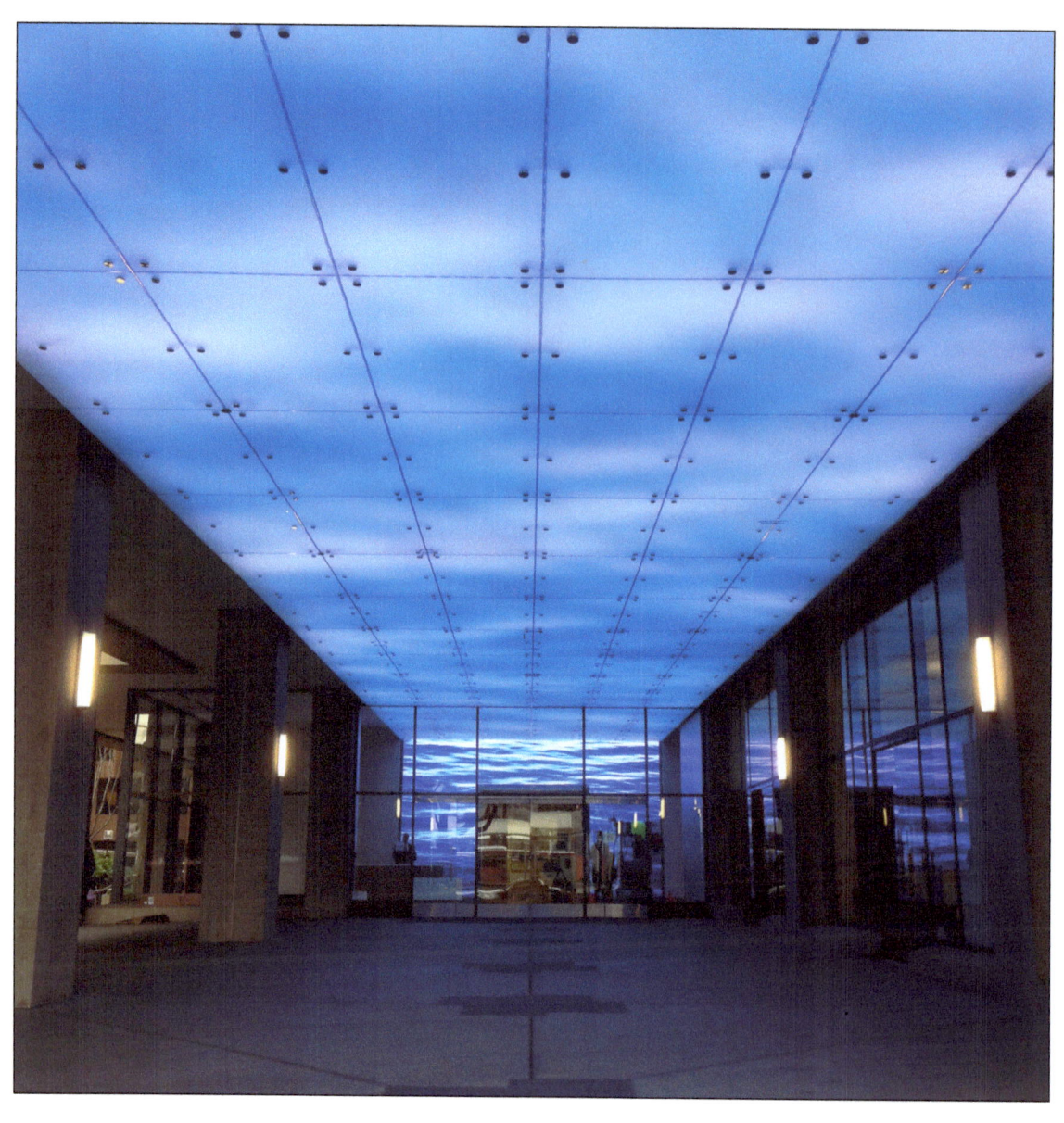

L: Hotel Oakland, Grandma's Home.
R: Hellman-Heller House, Pacific Heights, San Francisco.

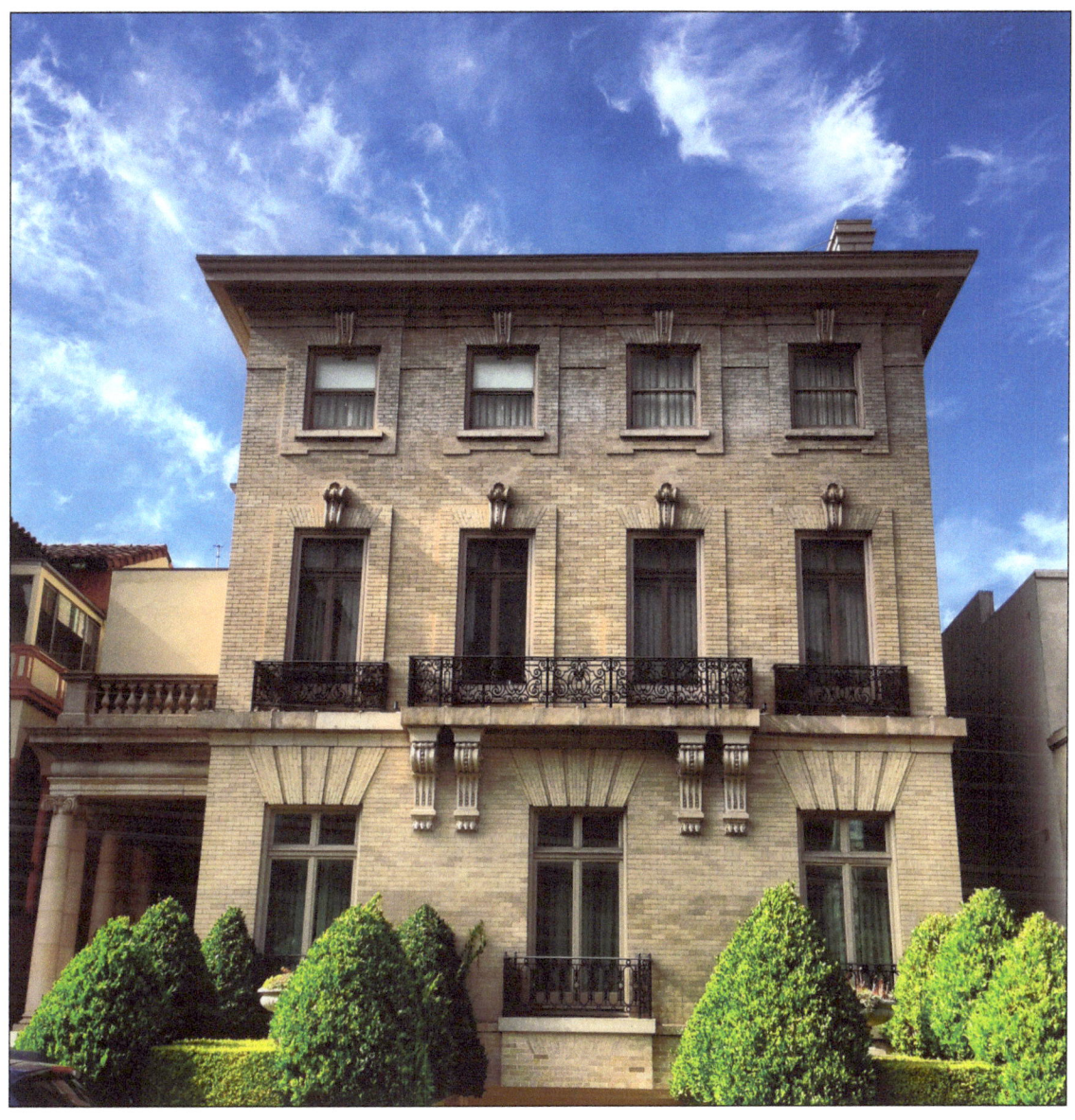

Some of us think holding on makes us strong; but
sometimes it is letting go.

—Herman Hesse

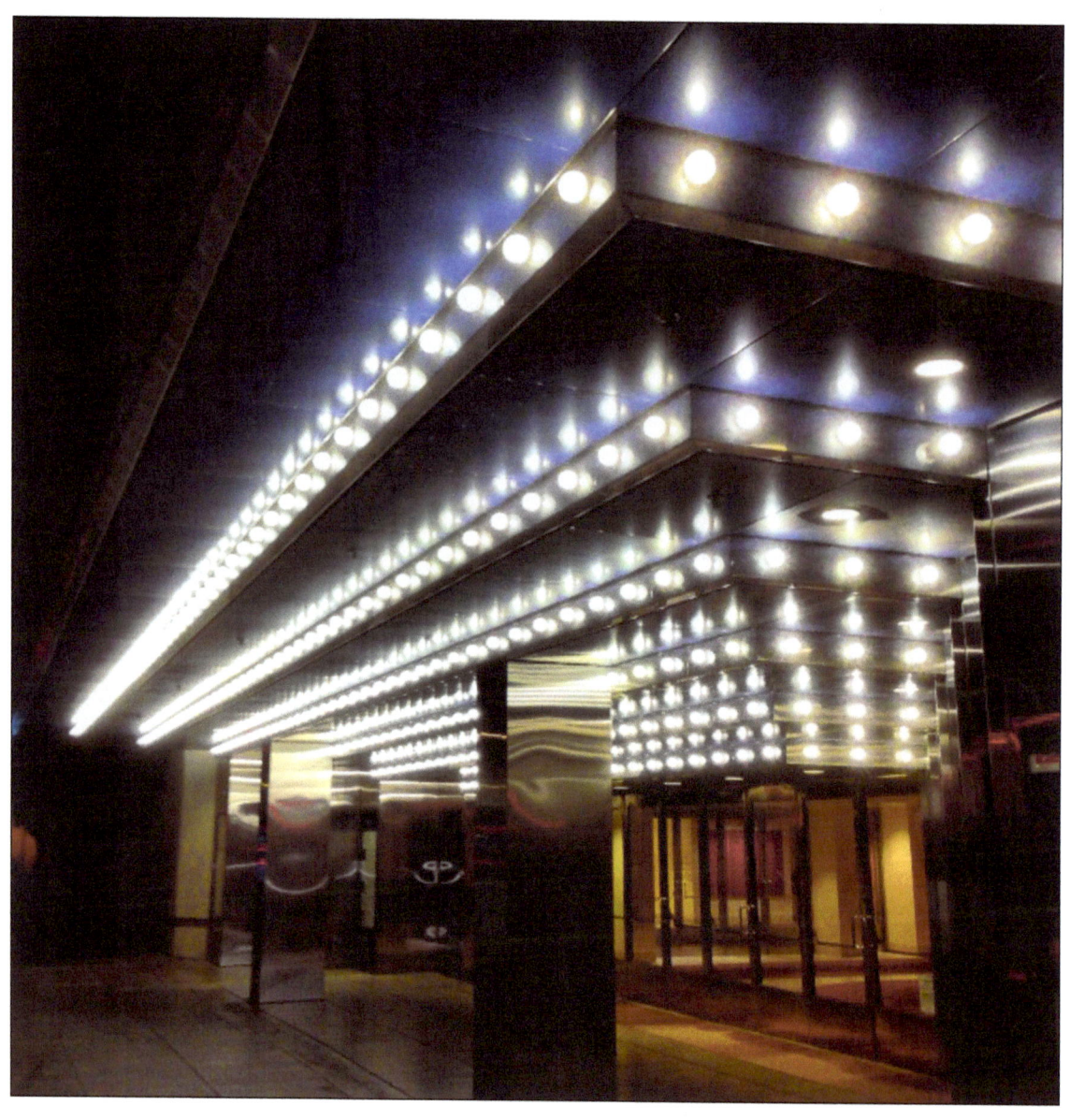

L: Louis M. Davies Symphony Hall, San Francisco.
R: Transamerica Building, San Francisco.

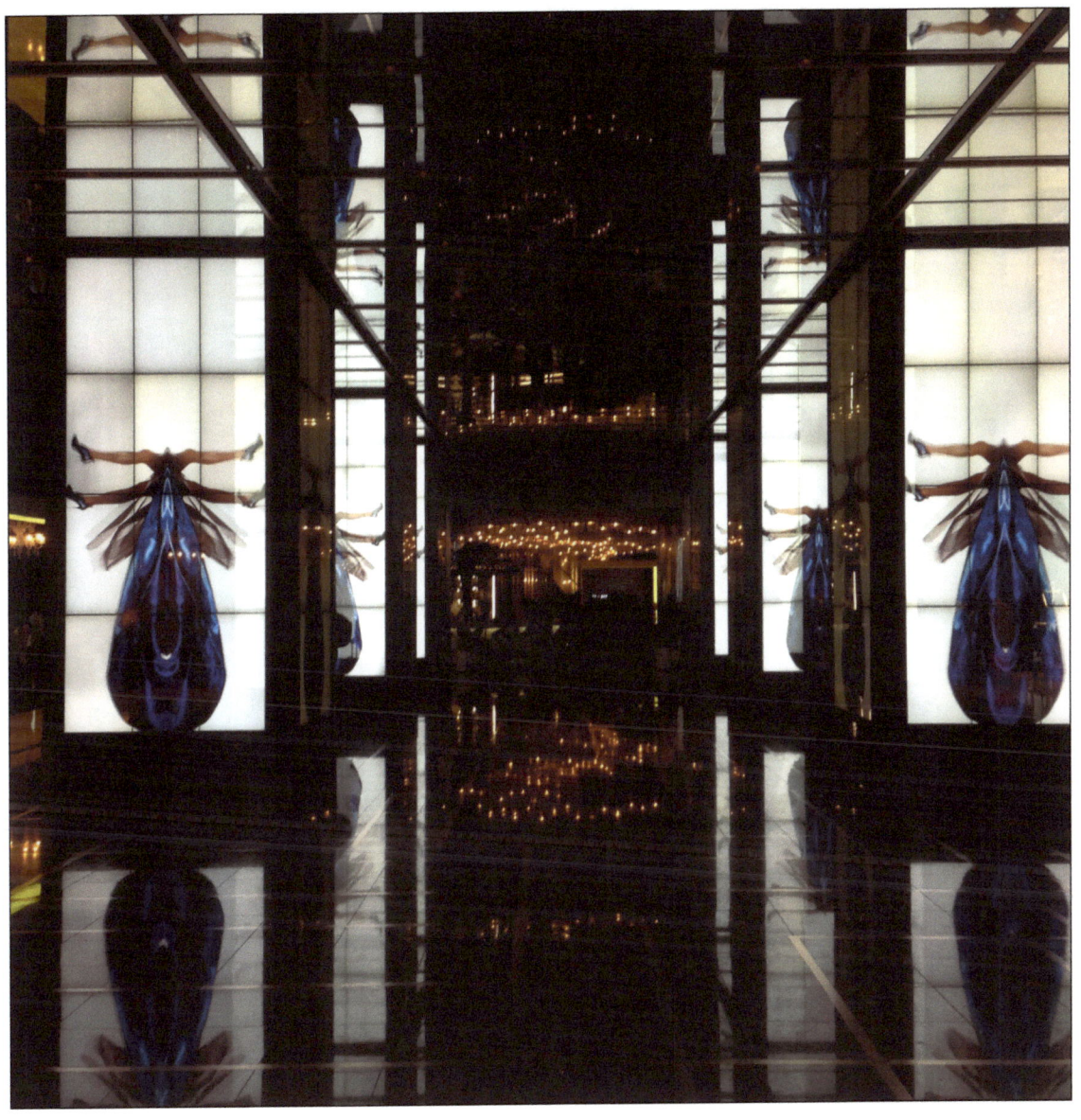

What people in the world think of you is really none
of your business.

—Martha Graham

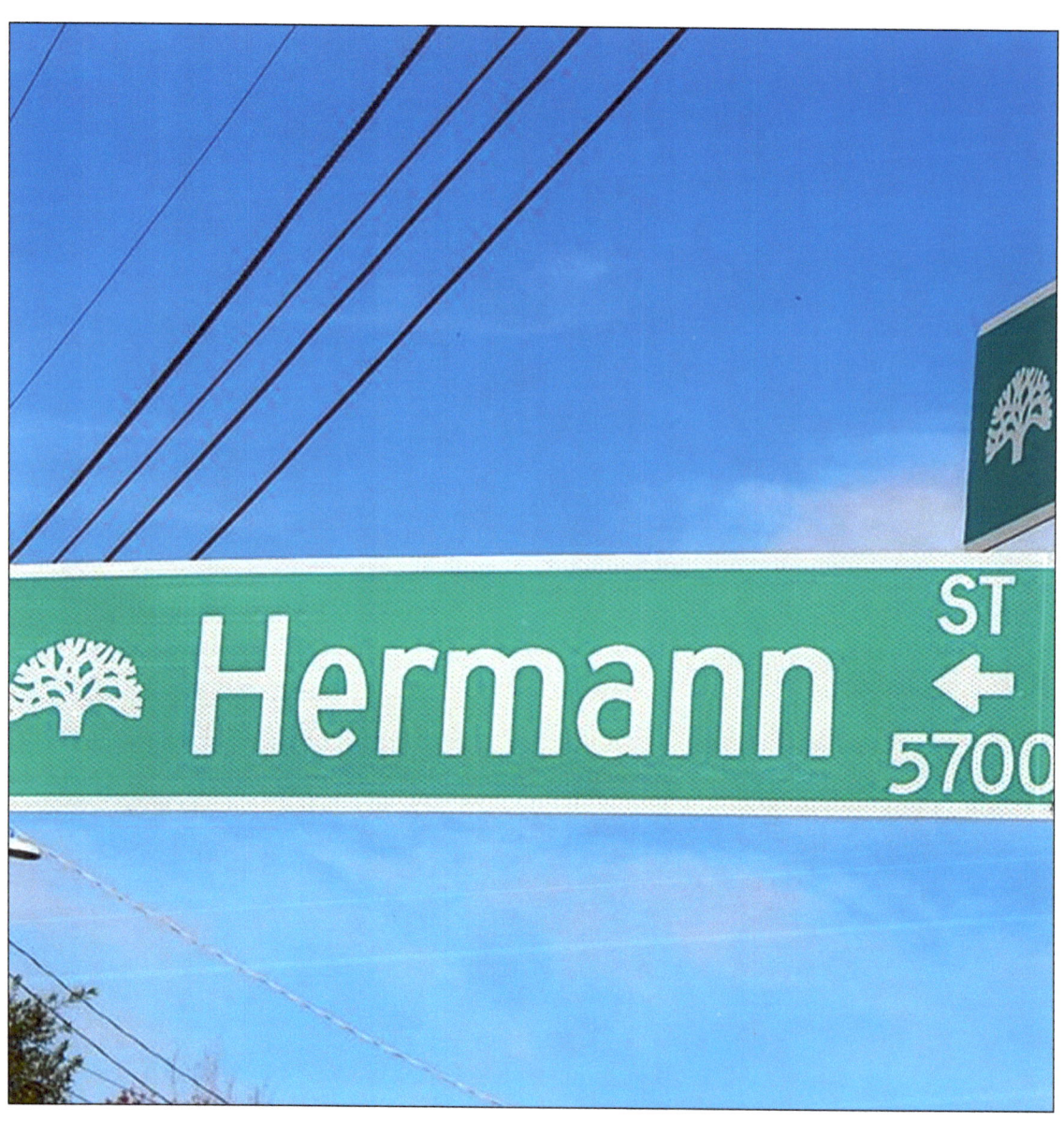

L: Rockridge, Oakland.
R: South of Market, San Francisco.

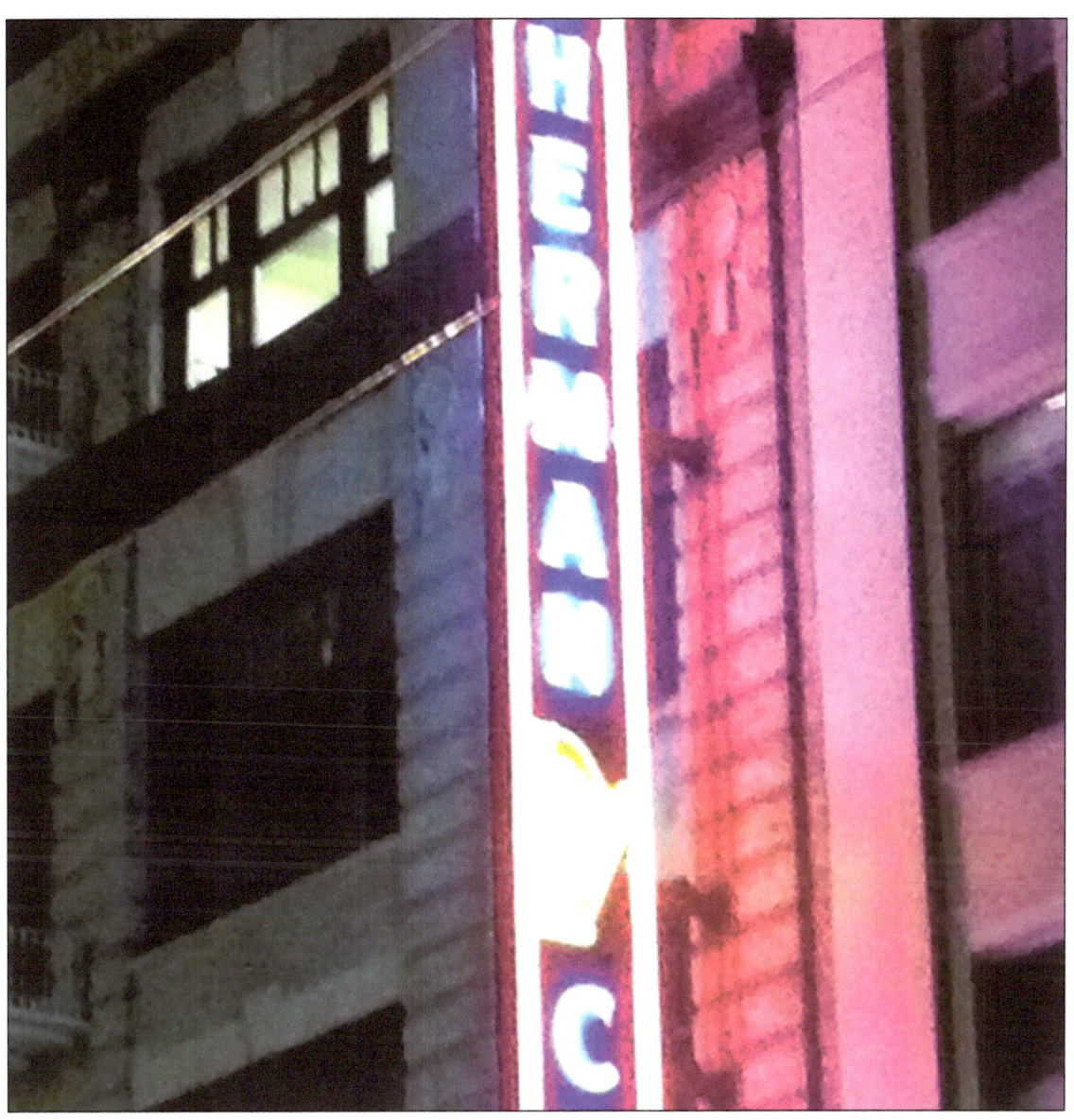

Be yourself. Everyone else is taken.

-—Oscar Wilde

ABOUT THE AUTHOR

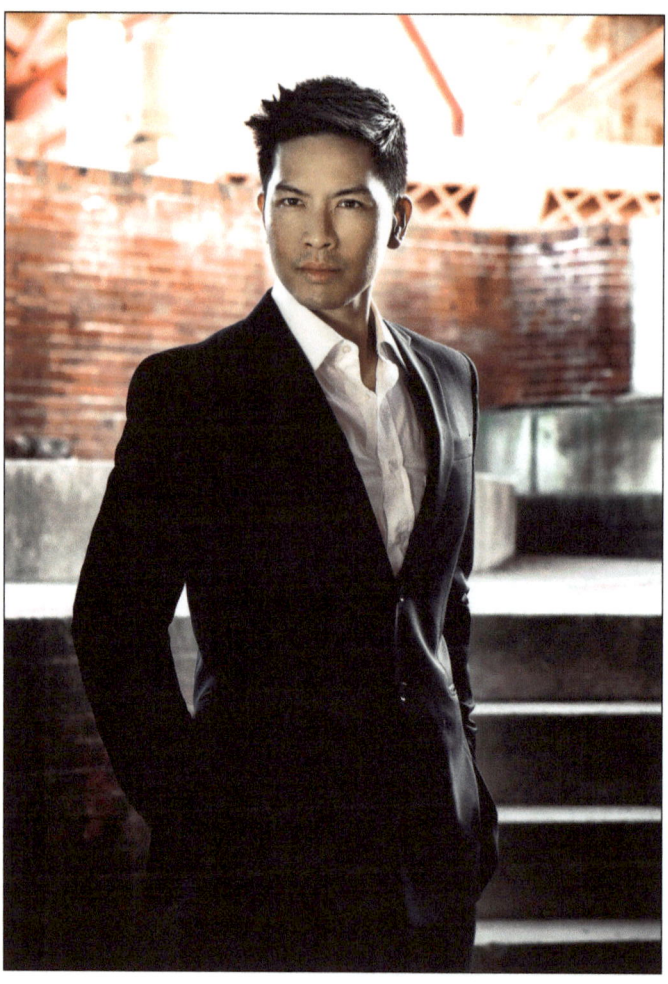

Herman Chan, born and raised in the San Francisco Bay Area, is a renowned Real Estate Broker and Media Personality. After graduating from UC Berkeley with a Mass Communication degree, Herman launched an illustrious career brokering deals for buyers and sellers. His hit blog HabitatForHermanity.com is read by thousands each day. He has appeared on countless TV shows and media outlets like HGTV, CNN Money, CBS & Huffington Post. Ranked in the "Top 50 Most Influential in Real Estate," Herman is a sought after public speaker around the world on the topics of branding, social media and real estate trends. In his free time Herman models part time and authored a book of his photography called LOOKING UP, which hit the best sellers list.

www.ingramcontent.com/pod-product-compliance
Lightning Source LLC
Chambersburg PA
CBHW040325190526
45162CB00008B/73